Lithium Jesus

Lithium Jesus

A Memoir of Mania

Charles Monroe-Kane

The University of Wisconsin Press

Heidi,

Love,

charles

The University of Wisconsin Press
1930 Monroe Street, 3rd Floor
Madison, Wisconsin 53711-2059
uwpress.wisc.edu

3 Henrietta Street, Covent Garden
London WCE 8LU, United Kingdom
eurospanbookstore.com

Printed in the United States of America

This book may be available in a digital edition.

Library of Congress Cataloging-in-Publication Data

Names: Monroe-Kane, Charles, author.
Title: Lithium Jesus: a memoir of mania / Charles Monroe-Kane.
Description: Madison, Wisconsin: The University of Wisconsin Press, [2016]
Identifiers: LCCN 2016012943 | ISBN 9780299310004 (cloth: alk. paper)
Subjects: LCSH: Monroe-Kane, Charles. | Broadcasters—United States—Biography.
| Mentally ill—United States—Biography.
Classification: LCC PN1990.72.M66 A3 2016 | DDC 791.4402/8092 [B]—dc23
LC record available at https://lccn.loc.gov/2016012943

This work is a memoir. It reflects the author's present recollections of his experiences
over a period of years. Some names and identifying details have been changed, and certain
individuals are composites. Dialogue and events have been recreated from memory, and
in some cases chronology has been sparingly compressed or rearranged for the benefit of
narrative clarity.

Dedicated to

Erika

(full stop)

In memory of my big brother

Joe Kane.

I love you man. You left way too goddamn soon.

Contents

Afterword

Epilogue

Contents

Acknowledgments

Thanks to Raphael Kadushin at the University of Wisconsin Press.

Thanks to Andrea Riley, Anne Strainchamps, Sara Nics, Katie McGlenn, and Jennifer Dargan. Your critiques of my first draft were invaluable.

Special thanks to my editor, Seth Jovaag. Without you there would be no book. I am forever grateful—all respect.

Prologue

* . * . * . * . * . *
. * . * . * . * . * .
* . * . * . * . * . *

The Voices

By the time you get to my age, you've experienced fear. A man with a gun. An acid trip gone wrong. A serious car accident. Holding a loved one's hand in the ICU. But there is something singular about the fear that comes from hearing voices. Voices no one can hear but you.

The first time I heard the voices, I was watching *BJ and the Bear* on TV with my siblings in the basement rec room next to the bedroom I shared with my older brother. It started with a humming in my left ear. Then came an airy sound, as though someone standing way too close to me had just inhaled. It grew louder still, like a box fan on medium speed, a little white noise. But from inside the whirring, spinning fan blades someone on the other side was now whispering what very well might have been my name.

I had been out of control all evening—talking incessantly, pissing off my brother and sister, standing while everyone else sat at the dinner table because there was no way I could hold still. My family was fed up with me, and it only got worse. I started spinning around and jumping over the couch, confused by the increasing volume of the sounds in my head. Finally, my mom said enough: off to my room. I crawled into the bottom bunk and cuddled up with Sir Bosley, my grandmother's Boston Bull Terrier that I claimed as my own, and strained to hear the show through the thin basement paneling.

The voices were getting kinetic now. I felt like I was on my Uncle Butch's speedboat on Mosquito Lake, when I would dangle over the edge, daring fate, skimming my hand on the fast moving water, the roar of the outboard motor so thick you couldn't actually talk to the person next to you. But as I lay motionless in my bed

3

the sound was being replaced by something else—faint voices, off in the distance, and they were clearly calling me.

I was scared. So fucking scared. And then all was still. Silent. Good. Even as a child I must have sensed it—the calm before the storm.

The Jesus Years

*   *   *   *   *
  *   *   *   *
*   *   *   *   *

Summer Camp Salvation

I'm so happy 'cause today
I've found my friends . . .
They're in my head.

Nirvana, "Lithium"

Don't talk like a fat man. Never get above your raisin'. And don't you ever, never ever, get played by the man. Because in my family, you can play anything you want: just don't play the sucker.

In theory, this made life for the Kane clan easy—we just didn't do anything. Working hard at a job, caring at all for it, got you teased at a family BBQ. You were a dupe at best, or worse, a sucker, if you got caught up in the fool's quest of chasing success, and a scarlet letter "S" would be forever on your forehead if your efforts were discovered. Only a moron would let themselves be bamboozled by the government, the military, a job, religion, or even college. Because in the end, the boss always got more out of it than you did. Be free by doing nothing: that was the Kane way.

Nearly as admirable were those who could make gobs of money for doing *almost* nothing, preferably in about twenty hours a week or less. Several years ago, after my wife had our second child, she left her high-powered sixty-hour-a-week job to become a part-time consultant. When my family heard what she charged per hour, they first thought she was joking. Then they glowed with Kane pride.

"They pay you to give your opinion?!" my dad crowed. "Fantastic!"

It was as though my wife had cured cancer.

This work-sucks philosophy, by latent design, meant everyone in my family was very poor. And in the rare instances when someone had two nickels to rub together, there was great pride taken in not doing so.

One summer, in the humid suck-your-soul stickiness of northeast Ohio, my uncles went Dumpster-diving and came back toting trash bags filled with thousands of greeting cards. For a few days, some of my cousins and I happily spent hours organizing them on my kitchen table into categories like birthdays, anniversaries, sympathy, and Christmas. The cards were then stored in my Aunt Lynette's basement, on a shelf next to Uncle Joe's multiple deep freezers of popsicles he'd pilfered from Dumpsters. For years afterward, various cousins and aunts and in-laws would swing by Lynette's to pick up a free greeting card for some "special occasion." Of course, since we had such a large family, most of the cards ended up going to each other. A greasy smudge on the envelope was a telltale sign. As was the "+1" handwritten next to the "9" on a card for your tenth birthday.

In the Kane mindset, every card you didn't buy represented another hour you didn't have to work. And every hour you didn't work was an act of rebellion against the system. This paradigm governed our lives. Another example: at an all-you-can-eat buffet, only a sucker eats bread.

"Don't be a dumbass, Chucky," my Uncle Dick told me the first time I walked into the local Ponderosa Steakhouse. "Make them pay for only charging $4.95 for a child's portion. Eat all the prime rib you can."

–––

My extended family, which is very large and close knit and entirely based in the Rust Belt of northeastern Ohio, falls into two camps: the stoic men and the brassy women. My uncles, my father, my male cousins, my older brother—these are men of few words. They hunt alone, drive long-distance trucks alone, and quietly tinker in the barn or over car engines alone. Their advice, when offered, is short and sweet. But more importantly, the men in my family are, almost without exception, deeply eccentric. Eccentricity, in fact, is lauded almost as much as not being a sucker. So when my namesake Uncle Chuck went hunting with only a bowie knife and turned up later dragging the body of an eight-point buck up his driveway during one of our many forty-plus-people Sunday dinners, no one was surprised. When Uncle Dick fired up his backhoe at four in the morning to dig yet another pond on his land, that was par for the course.

One summer during my middle school years, my Uncle Joe moved into a homemade teepee he'd built in his backyard. For his own entertainment, he later dug a six-by-six-foot pit next to it and filled it with old oil and rancid meat he collected nightly from Dumpsters and then set fire to the whole mess. Later, as the pit cooled, he watched from his teepee as animals picked through the smoking remains. This was "entertainment." Even though he barely spoke to us kids, we'd hang out in his yard and watch him light his fires or shower outside with his clothes on while we methodically munched our way through his enormous stash of popsicles someone else had deemed garbage.

Though they didn't talk much, the men in my family were a blast. From stealing wood off government property to spontaneously going for a two-day walk, they were always up to something. They let us shoot guns and drive three-wheelers. They built us forts and go-carts. For fun, Uncle Butch and Uncle Joe filled garbage bags with nitromethane, a liquid explosive that contains twice the energy per volume of gasoline. This was Butch's domain, as he was a professional drag racer who once bested the legendary Shirley Muldowney at the Gator Nationals, and nitromethane was the fuel he used. They strung a long wick to the garbage bags and the ensuing explosion was the granddaddy of all booms, even better than when they tied M80s to thick metal bolts and blasted fish out of ponds, another pastime. They had to give the hobby up, however, when static electricity from one of the bags sparked an early explosion, sending both men to the hospital.

The ladies were a different breed entirely. While the men quietly retreated to their garages, basements, or tents after a

Sunday dinner, the women—all large, big breasted, and loud—would cackle in the kitchen, telling bawdy tales while elbow-deep in dishes or baking flour. I gravitated toward them—my mother, my grandmother who moved in with us when I was a toddler, my aunts Mary, CoAnne, Lynette, and Noreen, not to mention my female cousins, ten of them, almost all much older than me. I found the volume of their dense chatter comforting. And I liked their advice, which came not in the form of stoic platitudes but through personal narratives. From an early age I was more interested in baking or shopping at flea markets than learning how to rebuild an engine. To this day I can make a birthday cake from scratch or an entire Thanksgiving meal without a recipe, but I can't change the oil in my car.

Still, the men had great influence on me, starting with my father, who was odd in his own way. His eccentricity manifested itself in moving. We moved all the time, and certainly not to advance my father's career. We took it for granted at the time, though I've since asked him why we moved so often. He said he didn't have much choice, that he simply had Gypsy blood. I remember my first time seeing real Gypsies. I was in Bucharest, and I saw two Gypsy women deftly steal a hard-boiled egg from an unsuspecting man on a tram. I followed them and watched as they peeled and ate that egg, laughing and talking. Their colorful clothes, their air of defiance and freedom—I wish my father had been with me. He would have liked them.

My older sister and brother moved fourteen times during their childhood and attended a new school every year from first grade to each of their senior years in high school. I moved ten times. Oklahoma. Northern Ontario. A bunch of places in Ohio that were always within a few hours of our extended family. To this day, my sister still resents all the moving we did. Me and my brother, however, went with the flow. We always kept empty boxes under our bed, ready to pack up for the next move. And we adapted, my brother by getting high in a variety of ways and me by making the whole thing a game.

I saw each new town as a stage upon which I could practice my act. When you move a lot growing up, you have to learn fast how to make friends. I was good at it. I could strike up a conversation with anyone, and I adopted a precocious, chubby, class-clown persona that served me well, plus I knew how to get (mostly) As, stay out of trouble, and deliver a timely "yessir" to principals and teachers to earn a seat in the smart-kid classes.

But I was a very strange kid. By the time I was ten or eleven, I would spend hours alone under my parents' bed squeezing and unsqueezing my hands, interlocking my fingers, and cutting off the circulation to my fingers and toes with rubber bands to feel them tingle. All the while I would listen to my "friends" in my head as they chattered to me—they had hauntingly weak little voices and sang or spoke in a language I mostly didn't understand. I found ways to toy with these utterings. I'd bend the noise by shaking my head back and forth or spinning in circles. I would hold my breath to silence them or drink soda and listen to them scream.

For the most part, I didn't worry much about the voices. But at night, things could get dicey. In my bed, the voices would circle me, and their chorus would become one. Then they would force me to leave my body and carry me to "the Island." Most nights we never made it to our destination. We just traveled and traveled—gliding inches above water and roads. But when we did arrive at the Island it was clear that somewhere on it lived the source of the voices—their leader, I suppose. The Source. I knew instinctively that He was to be avoided at all costs.

In desperation, I found that self-mutilation brought temporary relief. I would scratch deep bloody lines into my knees at night or rip off pieces of my toenails until they bled.

But when the voices would peak and start to scare me and my knees and nails were too painful to scratch and pick, I developed a new tactic. As the voices started to circle I would pick my nose—hard. So hard it would bleed. The sight and feel of the blood would bring me back to my room, where it was quiet again. I never told my parents about the voices, and to avoid suspicion about the blood from my laundry-doing mother, I began going to bed shirtless. I would sit up and bleed freely over my bare chest—night after night. When the voices faded I would clean up quietly and get a good night's sleep. By the time I was thirteen, however, the habit had destroyed the inside of my nose, and I had to get both nostrils cauterized. Thus eliminating my best defense against the Source.

At school, the voices were less frequent, but when they did appear I developed a new method to deal with them and my ever-increasing mania. It was a game I later named "facetious deep-freeze." Here's how it worked:

First, as the teacher spoke, I would pick out a single long word or short phrase and separate the vowels from the consonants. The rule was that this could only be done with my fingers, no paper allowed. My left hand would count the vowels, my right the consonants.

Points were awarded for equal vowel and consonant combinations. For example: "Never again" would be ten points, as it has five vowels and five consonants. You would be surprised how many times this occurs when you pay attention. No points were awarded for any word or word combinations that did not contain at least five vowels and five consonants.

I would move my fingers constantly as my teachers spoke, keeping score in my head and memorizing the phrases. I still remember the moment I discovered the word "deepfreeze." D-P-F-R-Z and E-E-E-E-E. (I gave that twenty-five points!) But nothing could compare to the day when my social studies teacher used the word "facetious." A-E-I-O-U in order! If only F-C-T-S was five consonants!

The game relaxed me greatly at school. But even with my coping mechanisms, my nights continued to give me problems. With the onset of puberty, I resorted to binge eating before bed. Somehow, sucking down a couple glasses of milk, a piece of chicken, and some mashed potatoes got me to sleep faster. This meant fewer trips to the Island. Still, at times, the voices would carry me. I somehow sensed that the Source wanted to see me. It was only a matter of time.

~~~

After years of moving, my parents made the decision to stay put in Southington, Ohio, for my high school years. By then, my brother was in the Army and my sister was in the Air Force, so it was just me and my mom and dad. We rented an old garage in a field. We had electricity and water but little else. It was on a dirt road, and there were no other houses nearby, just tall grasses and scrubby trees. Makeshift walls of two-by-four studs and plywood that didn't even reach the ceiling separated my folks' bedroom from the rest of the structure's square footprint. My dad cobbled together a loft for me above the washer and dryer. It wasn't much, but it was something, I guess. And our newfound stability gave me a chance to make a stab at going to college.

I did very well in high school and attracted the attention of a guidance counselor, who told my parents I had a shot at an academic scholarship. We were broke. No one in my family had ever gone to college. This was my chance.

―――

Early in high school, I rode the bus, a hellish forty-five-minute commute that began at 6:30 a.m. But the Fates would bless me. After a couple of weeks, a flirty and talkative farm girl with a pony-tail and wit began sitting on the bench across from me. Tammy favored button-down shirts that would part at the buttons, expos-ing the most glorious, creamy cleavage any horny thirteen-year-old boy could ask for. My Aunt Mary would say, "It's not fair that Chucky has to ride the bus that long." But those rides became the highlight of my life.

Near the end of our freshman year, Tammy, whose boobs continued to blossom, invited me to a summer camp organized by her church. The thought of a week spent sleeping in cabins, canoeing, sitting by campfires, and seeing her in a swimsuit— maybe a bikini!—tantalized me. Of course, I accepted.

Her church, however, was not cooperative. It was Pentecostal, and while we did swim and make s'mores, their dress code required the girls to cover up their swimsuits with T-shirts and shorts.

Worse, by the end of the first day, Tammy had paired off with an older boy, a senior. Meanwhile, for the "unsaved" like me, the pressure grew increasingly intense as the week wore on. Everyone was talking to me about Jesus. Among the young campers, much of the buzz centered on the final night's tent revival service, where Preacher Randy was going to deliver a fire-and-brimstone message direct from God himself. "If you ain't saved after that, Satan's won you," a lanky kid told me during a canoe ride. I could hear Uncle Joe in my head saying "religion is for suckers." But I didn't tell the kid that.

The air was muggy and electric with cicada songs when the reverend began his sermon. Honestly, his oratorical style reminded me less of what I thought a man of God would sound like than it did the between-match rants delivered by the professional wrestlers I watched on Saturday mornings. The revelations and the gnashing of teeth left me mostly confused. Nonetheless, I was entranced. Then began the altar call, the time for the unsaved to approach the front of the tent to accept Christ into their heart. It dawned on me that this was *my* time, that others were probably expecting me to "do right" and bow and scrape my way to the front of the tent to prostrate myself before God. But I didn't want to do that. Did I? Wasn't that just playing the sucker?

The warm air soon began to hum with a cacophony of "thank you, Jesus" and mutterings in strange languages. I found it scary yet familiar. As the volume and intensity of the audience's intonations rose, I started to hear them, sprinkled in among the tongues—the voices had arrived. It damn near froze me in fear. For the first time, the voices were not from my own head but from the mouths of those around me. The mutterings became shouts; a handful of people began running up and down the aisles. Soon, it seemed, the chorus had circled me.

A man next to me, apparently in a trance, was overcome and fainted. The preacher knelt by him, microphone in hand, and declared him "slain in the spirit." I thought he was dead. But then the most amazing thing happened. He awoke and proclaimed, "I saw him. I saw him."

That was enough for me. I walked to the altar. I don't know why. I think I felt at home in some odd way for the first time in my life. The preacher put his hands on both my shoulders, looked into my eyes and asked me why I was here tonight. I told him I wanted to know the Source. He told me that if I got on my knees and accepted Jesus as my personal Lord and Savior all would be revealed to me. At that moment, as I dropped to my knees, there was only quiet. And then, in a whispered chorus, the voices transported me to the shores of the Island. And there, alone, I saw the Light. I met the Source. It was as if Jesus had been waiting there for me, and me for him, my entire life. As they say, "It was a peace that passeth all understanding." There was no fear as he bathed me in his blood and anointed me with his Spirit. Upon my return I faced the congregation with hands raised and tears streaming down my face.

"Hosanna, Hosanna! Halleluiah!" they shouted, as I spoke out loud—for the first time—in the language of the voices in my head.

The White Suit

Rockin' the world for you, Holy One,
Rockin' the world for you, and your son.
Stryper, "Rockin' the World"

I knew at the exact moment of my salvation that those voices were not in my head. They were a gift. That I, Chuck Kane, a fourteen-year-old American boy, was anointed by God as his special emissary—that God was speaking directly to me. I felt like the old me had been both obliterated and expanded and that my reformation was a miracle of Jesus.

Within days—and without telling my parents what I was up to—I was in Preacher Randy's office at Southington Life, the only church in town, trying to discover what I was supposed to do with all this newfound holiness. He quickly confirmed everything I felt—that I was special, that I was chosen by God, and most importantly that it was my duty to share the Good News with others.

But first, the sacraments. My baptism was held the following Sunday. Southington's baptismal was the size of a hot tub and stood stage left in front of the worship hall. I donned a scratchy white robe and, while Preacher Randy addressed the congregation, I looked into the water and had a vision of myself filling it with the damned. Even before I stepped in, I had the sensation of floating; I was high on Jesus.

Preacher Randy and I stepped into the water together. He clutched the back of my neck, pulled me to him, and pinched my nose shut with his other hand. "In the name of the Father!" he shouted, and down I went, the last few remaining scales being washed from my eyes. "In the name of the Son!" and he dunked me again, my loins girded with the truth of Christianity. "And in the name of the Holy Ghost!" and down I went the last time. I was baptized. The Source had fitted me with a new suit of armor.

With that, I was quickly confirmed into the church—a church that was to become the bedrock of my life for the rest of my high school years.

Southington Life was not Evangelical or Pentecostal or even overly charismatic, but "gifts of Spirit," such as speaking in tongues, were a regular occurrence, as were altar calls at the end of each service. The church took the King James version of the Bible literally, and its fundamental tenet was the possibility of salvation through Jesus, summed up in the oft-quoted John 3:16: "For God so loved the world, that he gave his only begotten Son, that whosoever believeth in him should not perish, but have everlasting life." Preacher Randy didn't spend much time on the love part; he was all about the perishing. In my life, I have seen many things done and said in the name of Jesus, but nobody could hit the fire and brimstone like Preacher Randy. He became my model for how to preach, and I mimicked him often in the years to come.

I spent hours alone in my room at home, praying for a sign from God that would tell me what to do. And then at a Wednesday night Bible study, I met a missionary named Mr. Johnson. He had just returned from Colombia, where he had set up a remote church in the jungle. With his eyes focused on some distant point over our heads, he told us of his family's narrow escape from a rebel group with the vaguely obscene name FARC. He told us how he fled the jungle with only the hand of God to guide him. Then he looked directly at me and said God had told him during their ordeal that there would be a prophet in Ohio who needed his help. That was why he was here, he said. "Are you that prophet?" he asked—a question that may have seemed rhetorical to the others but was like a horsewhip across my cheek.

A few months later, Mr. Johnson arranged for me to join an evangelical teen organization called MOI—Missions Outreach Incorporated—based in Bethany, Missouri. They sent small groups of teens around the globe to assist missionaries. To prepare the assistants, MOI ran a summer program that consisted of two weeks in Bethany for training, followed by eight weeks in the field. I applied and was accepted; I was to join a team that would work for an elderly American couple in the Philippines. God had answered my prayers. But first, I needed money: $3,000 to cover my expenses. I had seven months to raise the funds.

So how does a working-class kid from a rundown steel mill town raise three grand? He preaches, baby! With Randy's guidance and support, I traveled each Sunday to Evangelical and Pentecostal churches in the area and told them about my mission from God to spread his way, truth, and light, to the heathens of the Philippines.

I am naturally charismatic, but my preaching style at this point was little more than a teenaged imitation of Randy and the many televangelists I idolized—Pat Robertson, Tammy Faye and Jim Bakker, Oral Roberts, Jerry Farwell, and the silver-haired Robert H. Schuller. At home I would stand, fully dressed in a suit and tie, watching the religious channel on our thirteen-inch black-and-white TV, mimicking them while adjusting our rabbit-ear antennae. I was not just playing pretend. I was practicing to be them. Besides parroting their words, I studied their hand movements, their pregnant pauses, and their use of the stage and the microphone. I paid special attention to how and when they chose to use the Bible, not only for its words but as a prop they would touch, pat, or hold above their head like a sword. The fuzzy reception on our TV added to the allure that this performance was coming from far away—that it was coming from God.

I also made sure to memorize a lot of Bible verses. I remember Randy telling me that if I ever ran out of something to say, I should just pause, pick up the Bible, and start quoting it at random.

My sermons were never theological dandies. I kept things super simple; I spoke of Jesus and eternal damnation of the un-saved. And then I punctuated my thoughts with scripture. I quickly learned when the audience's attention was focused on me, and over time I learned how to hold that focus for longer, to tease it out and use it.

Perhaps the real power of my sermons simply derived from the fact that someone so young was up there on stage, driven by the strength of his convictions. Maybe the people in the congregation wished I was their son or grandson. Maybe they vicariously misremembered themselves through me. My narrative gave them every reason to do so. I told them about the voices and my experience with the Source. I told them how God, acting through Mr. Johnson, had selected me as a prophet. In church after church, it worked. "He is chosen!" they would yell with hands waving in the air. I ended all my sermons the same way: an altar call—a time when the unsaved could come forward to accept Jesus or the saved-but-not-right-with-the-Lord crowd could kneel at the altar while others prayed over them. This was the "hard sell," especially for the unsaved.

And it was during the altar calls that the offering plate quietly went around. Soon I had the money I needed.

—◆—

I was a good kid. I didn't drink, I didn't smoke, I didn't have sex, I got As and volunteered. My parents were proud of me and pretty much let me do whatever I wanted. But I was never sure what they thought of my newfound religion. So before I went, my newest, most important mission became having my family accept Jesus Christ as their personal Lord and Savior. They, too, would be washed in his blood.

Soon after my baptism, I ordered dozens of Christian-themed leaflets through the church from a company called Chick Publishing. They were, essentially, comic strips that always ended with a highly manipulative plea for salvation. On the back side were blank spaces to write out church information or a phone number in case you were passing them out to strangers. I'd leave these leaflets in my parents' newspaper or tucked under their plates at dinner. I used the blank spaces to write special messages to them: "I love you too much to see you burn in hell!" or "All I want for my birthday this year is for you to accept Jesus."

I cajoled them, too, turning every conversation toward the warmth that could be found in God's love and the fires of hell that awaited nonbelievers. I'm not really sure why I was so fixated on making my parents believe in Jesus. The obvious answer is that I wanted them to be spared from hell, which was a very real place to me. But I think I also saw their conversion as a test of my new faith: if I was to be pure, then my family must be so, too.

My parents grew more curious as my fervor grew, and they started attending church with me more often. Over time, I backed off from overt proselytizing, opting instead to lead by example. By not lying. By living pure. By reading my Bible at the dining room table. By praying for hours in my room with my door open.

It took a few years, but the seeds I planted eventually took root. My senior year in high school, I saw an ad in our church bulletin: they were hiring a part-time janitor. My dad had recently lost his job—again—so I told him about it. He was interested, but he didn't think he qualified because he wasn't a Christian. I told him he should at least meet Randy and ask. I introduced them, and they totally hit it off. There was no religious litmus test, and my dad was hired.

Within a year, I was off to college, and my parents decided to take a month-long trip to Alaska to visit my sister. While hiking on a glacier outside Anchorage, my dad felt, as he put it later, "the awe of God." And it set him on his heels. Then, on the plane ride home, a man in the seat next to him witnessed about Jesus, "just like Chucky did."

Soon after, my parents closed the deal. My mother, who considered herself a closeted Christian, reaffirmed her faith. And my father accepted Jesus Christ as his personal Lord and Savior. That fall, on their twenty-fourth wedding anniversary, my parents were baptized and remarried as Christians. I gave my mother away at the altar.

But they didn't stop there. During their last visit to Alaska, my parents had met a man at my sister's church who owned a rundown fishing camp on Hitchenbrook Island in Prince William Sound, a place with no electricity or running water. The man had always dreamed of turning this remote outpost into a ministry, an island of respite where Christian leaders could recharge. From the moment they were baptized, my parents felt called by God to run this camp. And one month later—as winter was setting in—they sold everything they owned in Ohio and moved to Alaska to do just that. They were on that island for two years and remained in Alaska for another ten, doing the work of God.

—m—

But before all that, I had had my own leap of faith to make. I was fifteen, I had raised the money to go to the Philippines, and now I was in Bethany, Missouri, donning the breastplate of righteousness, the belt of truth and the shield of faith. Mission Outreach Incorporated's two-week training was the moment I'd been waiting for—the moment when I would finally strap on the armor of God for spiritual battle.

MOI wasn't your typical summer camp. First, there were a lot of kids like me, maybe fifty altogether, who were egotistical, type-A, aggressive child preachers on a mission from God. We all wanted to out-Jesus each other. During sunrise exercise drills, we high-stepped through tires, clambered over slatted wooden walls, crawled under barbed wire, and scampered up ropes while one of the strident college-student counselors shouted the chapter and verse numbers of scripture passages that we, as a group, had memorized the day before. "Matthew 28:19!" Only the losers would fail to bellow back, fully confident, "Go ye therefore, and teach all nations, baptizing them in the name of the Father, and of the Son, and of the Holy Ghost."

Forgetting a verse could cost you twenty push-ups, ten burpees, or some other physical punishment. Worse, the others would silently scorn you. At the conclusion of one particularly grueling run in combat boots and full backpacks, an aggressive female counselor locked eyes with me and yelled "Acts 1:8!" I was panting and could feel the eyes of the campers on me. But I was ready. The New Testament was hammered into me like the nails through

Christ's hands, and I busted out the verse with the power of a prophet on the eve of the Second Coming: "But ye shall receive power, after the Holy Ghost is come upon you: and ye shall be my witnesses unto me both in Jerusalem, and in all Judea, and in Samaria, and unto the uttermost part of the earth." Then I bellowed "Amen!" over and over again as I sprinted back to the cabins.

After morning workouts came personal devotions, breakfast, and a passionate, tent-revival-style sermon. After lunch it was language (for me, Tagalog) and "cultural study," which taught us culturally sensitive ways to witness. (After all, you don't want to offend the person you're trying to save from eternal damnation). The rest of the day alternated between physical exercise and preaching, though during the afternoons we were afforded a brief period of free time. This time, however, was the most nerve wracking. Elders in the camp would, without warning, ask to meet with an individual camper for the all-important "discernment," during which they would decree whether you had a particular gift of the spirit. You never knew when your day was coming. The feeling of anticipation was part Christmas Eve, part waiting to get paddled by the vice principal. "What if I'm found unworthy?" we whispered. Most campers, it was rumored, were told they had no gift at all.

We all knew the verse: 1 Corinthians 12:8–10, the description of the gifts of the Holy Spirit: "For to one is given by the Spirit the word of wisdom; to another the word of knowledge by the same Spirit; To another faith by the same Spirit; to another the gifts of healing by the same Spirit; To another the working of miracles; to another prophecy; to another discerning of spirits; to another diverse kinds of tongues; to another the interpretation of tongues."

The last gift I wanted to be tagged with was the ability to interpret as others spoke in tongues. Almost as bad was "discerning spirits," which sounded totally lame. I prayed that they would see in me a miracle worker or a prophet, but I most feared I would be deemed giftless. Then one afternoon, while sunning myself on a dock overlooking the small lake at Missions Hill Ranch, I heard footsteps. I squinted up and saw the outline of a man in a blue-grey suit. It was my time.

The man walked me to the camp's beautiful little country chapel, inside of which another half-dozen men stood waiting. He closed the door and sat me in a chair in the center of the room. In unison, the men closed in and laid their hands on me. They started praying and, for what seemed like a sweat-soaked eternity, spoke in tongues. They became ecstatic. Finally, one man seized me by both shoulders and shook me hard. "Go out and heal in the Spirit!"

Heal? I experienced a brief pang of disappointment; miracles and prophecy were out. Being a faith healer also seemed like a bit much for me, something only Christ himself could manage. Honestly, I didn't know what to think. I knew one thing, though: I wouldn't be sending any postcards home about it. "Hey Mom and Dad, camp is great. Ticks are terrible though (but not as bad as the food! ☺). By the way, I'm a faith healer now! Miss you all! Love in Jesus, Chucky."

—⁓—

I lived in Oklahoma for a year when I was in sixth grade. When I was nine, my family spent a summer in Ontario. I'd been to Disneyland. Add a bunch of places in Ohio to the list and that was the extent of what I'd seen of the world in my first fifteen years. So when I stepped into the humid 110-degree air of chaotic Manila and boarded a flamboyantly decorated open-air jeepney, I was floored. We hurtled past vendors and filth and water running in the streets and military vehicles. I prayed so hard it almost hurt. I was scared. I wanted to go home. And yet . . . Jesus suffered and died at Calvary to save me from my sins. What was I willing to endure for him?

Six of us, plus a college-aged counselor, had traveled together from MOI to the Philippines. We stayed for our first few days in a pretty Spanish colonial villa owned by our host church in a rural suburb of the city. We relaxed. We ate amazing food. We saw monkeys and snakes and lizards and more large insects and other animals than I had ever seen at the Cleveland Zoo. We swam in the nearby river and got used to the heat and another language and culture.

After those restful days, I was invited to spend some time alone with the Petersons, our missionary host family. They were Texans who had lived in the Philippines for more than thirty years. Their church's base camp was a jungle outpost about thirty minutes north of Quezon City. The mission also had small satellite churches all over the main island, Luzon. Their largest ministry and church was in Olongapo, near the Subic Bay U.S. Naval Base. This massive base was, at the time, America's second largest foreign military installation (second only to Clark Air Force Base just north of it). Olongapo had become a de facto prostitute city and debauchery central for U.S. service members on R&R.

On his wraparound front porch, the railings thick with jungle vines and exotic plants, Pastor Peterson and I bowed our heads and prayed together, and the Lord made clear his orders: the two of us would leave the others from MOI behind and spend a few days together in Olongapo. We'd leave in the morning.

"If God ain't gonna destroy this Sodom and Gomorrah, then I guess we better get down there and save it," he said. Buoyed by faith and prayer, my hesitation and fear dissipated. I was ready for my close up.

"By the way," he added. "We'll be joined by some of the Guerrillas for God."

***

Back at our base camp, the MOI team's mission, ostensibly, was to build a vocational school for dozens of down-and-out Amerasian boys ranging in age from nine to fifteen. As Mr. Peterson explained, these were the sons of U.S. service members and Olongapo prostitutes. Before coming to Jesus, the boys had lived on the streets, abandoned by their American fathers and scorned by their society. Many had turned to glue huffing and petty crime. Their mothers were mostly Catholic and thus did not use contraception — even with their johns. Once these boys agreed to accept Jesus into their hearts, Mr. Peterson would invite them to the base camp and give them three square meals a day, some basic job training, a roof over their heads, and an opportunity to learn how to witness to and save others like them. The boys were rough, lean, and quick to fight. They were also hard working, loud, and streetwise to a fault. They all wore hand-me-down U.S. Army camouflage. These were the Guerrillas for God. I was enthralled.

The cinder block school we eventually finished with the guerrillas—and they worked at least as hard as we did, mixing mortar in five-gallon buckets and scampering up ladders with heavy cinder blocks balanced on their shoulders—was nice. But it was clear that the bulk of our energy was to be directed at street preaching. Our goal, after all, was to save the local heathens. Which was fine by me. I was a terrible brick mason.

So it was that Mr. Peterson and I, together with a few guerrillas, made our first trip to his church in Olongapo, a roughly ninety-minute journey we would end up repeating two or three times a week for the remainder of my stay there. The boys were to serve as my support staff. They would pass out tracts in Tagolog and English, explaining what it meant to be "born again" to anyone in the crowd who would listen.

When we arrived, the first thing Mr. Peterson did was take me to a tailor to be fitted for a suit. And what a suit it was—a white three-piece silk outfit offset by a maroon silk shirt with matching white cuffs and collar. A thin gold chain connected the lapels. For shoes, he ordered white wingtips.

Duly armored, I wasn't nervous at all the first time I walked up the dozen stairs to the large porch entrance of his church. Unlike the ornate cathedrals that dotted the cities and countryside of this predominately Catholic country (the Philippines boasts the third largest population of Catholics in the world after Brazil and Mexico, yet Mr. Peterson did *not* consider a Catholic saved) this church was simple, practical, and sturdy. "Four walls and a cross, Chucky. That's all you need. Jesus will do the rest."

It was a hot, rainy afternoon when I first stepped to the microphone stand wired to a twenty-watt amp perched at the edge of the stairs, a large wooden cross hanging on the wall behind me. I held the microphone in one hand and a Bible over my head with the other (a pose I'd learned from Preacher Randy) and started in. Though I'd learned a few phrases of conversational Tagalog during my MOI training, Mr. Peterson assured me that English was basically the lingua franca around here. If all else fails, he said with an assured wink, remember that God's message is "a truth that passeth all understanding."

It seemed to work. I witnessed for hours. Tired prostitutes would listen for a while and then walk on. Women carrying large bundles of food would set down their wares and take a chair. Men with fighting cocks in cages would light a cigarette and watch me work. It was hot in that suit, and the air smelled like street-vendor food—fresh popcorn, grilled monkey meat, and deep-fried everything. Then the stifling wind would shift and carry in odors of fresh urine or stagnant water. I wore sweet jasmine flowers on my lapel. I remember smelling them as I bowed my head on that first day when a young woman knelt on the stairs before me and accepted Jesus. Another notch on the belt—missionary style.

—————

Back at camp, the missionaries, as well as the other Anglos from the church, were largely segregated from the local Filipinos and the Guerrillas for God. While we slept in comfy beds, the guerrillas slept in a dirt-floor barracks in the villa's backyard, their hammocks covered by mosquito netting. One of their daily chores was to pick coconuts for us and whack the top off with machetes so we could drink the milk. The servile relationship didn't sit well with me. I felt a need to earn the boys' respect, and one day I made inroads by climbing (*sans* ropes) a tree to pick out my own coconut. When I came down, their slaps on my back emboldened me to ask Mr. Peterson if I could move in with them, even for just a short while. He reluctantly agreed.

I loved sleeping in that hammock. I felt holy, like I was living as Christ would, with the bedraggled and downtrodden. And I simply liked hanging out with the guerrillas: they were more fun. My fellow missionaries' complaints about the food and the heat and lack of "proper accommodations" irritated me. I suppose I felt a stab of self-righteous anger, too. I could tell they'd never had to pour water on their cereal because their family couldn't afford milk, that they didn't know what it was like to be poor like I did.

Within days, however, came my proper initiation. In the light of a full moon I was roughly awakened, dragged from my hammock, and taken to a small vegetable garden behind the barracks. There the boys, in silence, formed a tight circle around me. The oldest marked an X in the ground with a shovel, then handed it to me. I started to dig. A couple feet down I hit something. I got on my knees, scooping away the loose soil with my fingers until I'd unearthed a clay pot. I pulled it out, set it on the ground, and after a quick glance at the other boys removed the lid. Inside was a reeking, small bundle wrapped in fermenting cabbage. I took it out, peeled away the cabbage, and found a duck egg. The boy who had given me the shovel now took the egg and carefully unshelled the top fourth of it before handing it back. I looked inside: an aborted duck embryo was swimming in what delicately could be called a broth of yolk and fluids. I was horrified. But I knew what I had to do. I looked to the moon, said a short prayer asking for deliverance from vomiting, and sucked the shell dry. The boys danced around me and patted my back as I chewed and gagged and smiled. I now had the natives on my side.

—⁓⁓—

I had been in the Philippines for about three weeks, avoiding any discussion of my discerned spirit gift of healing, when Mr. Peterson invited me one day to preach the Sunday sermon inside his Olongapo church. This was a step up from street preaching, and I came ready. I delivered what I thought was a powerful sermon from the book of Daniel (my favorite book of the Bible). Channeling the prophet, at one point I slapped an inner wall of the church and wrote there, in white chalk, "Mene, mene, tekel, upharsin."

"This is *your* handwriting on the wall!" I hollered at the ever-growing crowd inside the church. I was venturing into some obscure biblical shit, but it didn't matter. I was feeling it. "Your days are numbered. Don't be Belshazzar!"

Then, during the altar call, it happened: a group of about a half-dozen men brought forward a woman, a cripple, who was laid out across a long board. They asked me to lay hands on her. To heal her. Apparently she was paralyzed from the waist down. *My God*, I thought, *they're serious.* I looked for Mr. Peterson and saw him in the crowd, staring at me, dead serious. He was waving his hand to the Lord, his half-Windsor knot soaked in sweat. *Are you for real, Chucky?* his gaze seemed to say.

I assumed Mr. Peterson knew about my alleged gift, but he had never brought it up, which was fine with me. Frankly, I was afraid of it. Part of me didn't believe it. I was open to the idea, but was it my life's calling to be a faith healer? That's pretty heavy stuff and, to be honest, it's a not exactly embraced as a "real job" by the world at large. But one doesn't have time to ponder such things when confronted, at age fifteen, with a crippled and crusty Filipino woman staring at you, waiting earnestly for your touch to fix her legs.

So here was my moment. The woman was there; the congregation had perked up. Many were standing now, screaming and clapping, and a few were striking gongs while others gave themselves over to glossolalia and ecstatic dancing. The heat and humidity rose from the cement floor. Sweat was pooling in circles on my already stained white suit. They were looking to me to heal her, to repair her broken body. But instead of boldly channeling some divine medicine, I felt myself begin to shake with fear, and suddenly I began to cry. Overcome, I squatted next to her, set the microphone on the ground and covered my face. Again, I felt a strong, familiar desire to be back home, to be back with my parents or playing basketball with my buddies, to hide from what was being asked of me. I don't know how long I waited there. I had to do something, but what?

I dropped my hands from my eyes and saw my palms were wet from tears. Inspiration struck. I straightened up and kneeled closer to the woman. I rubbed my wet hands first on her knees, then moved them to her forehead. I don't know what compelled me, but I drew myself up into a low crouch and then pressed down, hard and sudden, forcing my weight onto her head while screaming out my own version of a barbaric yawp. We waited. The room silenced. And then the woman rose to her feet and started to sing a Filipino Christian folk song that the Guerrillas for God had taught me just a few nights earlier:

Buhay, buhay, buhay kailan pa man
Si Hesus ay buhay
Buhay kailan pa man
Buhay, buhay, buhay kailan pa man
Si Hesus ay buhay kailan pa man.

Awitin natin ang aleluya
Si Hesus ay buhay kailan pa man
Awitin natin ang aleluya
Si Hesus ay buhay
Si Hesus ay buhay
Si Hesus ay buhay!

As the congregation joined her in song there were murmurs of "It's a miracle" and "She's healed!" My throat constricted. Many now were speaking in tongues. Everyone had their hands in the air. They were ecstatic. It became hard for me to breathe. "Halleluiah" they yelled, "Halleluiah." I ducked out through a side door and unceremoniously vomited on a patch of grass, nearly passing out. Thus endeth my first faith healing.

—‹‹‹‹—

That event haunted me for days, and about a week later I decided to hand my faith-healing doubts over to the Lord in prayer. First, I would fast for twenty-four hours. But as the hours wore on I could hear the voices in my head grow louder and more clear, to the point where they'd physically startle me. I retreated to a private room and closed the door. I wanted to hear them out. As their chorus of odd and familiar sounds began in earnest again, something different happened—the mutterings became syllables. And those syllables became words. "Chuck?" they said. "Chuck?"

Why the question mark? I wondered.

As they continued, I began to panic, and the fear morphed into a pain that settled into my chest. The fear of hearing actual words and not just sounds was overwhelming. I had a sense that something in me—my soul or my sanity—was ripping apart. The mania was upon me again. I ripped my shirt and, in a rage, started banging my head on the floor until it bled. Then in a fevered moment I stopped and I rested my cheek on the cool cement floor below me. I calmed my breathing and listened: "Chuck?" "Chuck?"

I waited. Ears ringing, I whispered to Jesus a new kind of prayer. "Jesus, I give up." *Jesus I give up.*

From that moment on, I decided that those Chucks with a question mark, which continued often, were not rebukes from an angry God. They were reminders from my Lord and Savior to remain steady on the path, reminders that Jesus was with me. Similar to the tribulations faced by all the great prophets, they were the thorn in my flesh—a gift from God I couldn't understand.

～～～

After that revelation my voice and my sermons began to grow stronger. I felt powerful. I continued to heal. Then one day Mr. Peterson told us that God had sent him a new vision. In our final two weeks, we were to travel to Hong Kong, which at the time was still a part of Great Britain, and smuggle Bibles into China. No preaching. No healing. Just smuggling. The word of God was the seed, and we were meant to plant it in Red China for the Godless Communists. God would do the rest. "But make no mistake," he added. "Your names will be written next to the commies who are saved in the Lamb's Book of Life on the day of harvest." And with that we ended our mission in the Philippines, waved goodbye to the Petersons, and boarded a plane for Hong Kong.

Following Mr. Peterson's instructions, we spent two anxious days in a youth hostel waiting to be contacted by our "host." Our counselor was a wreck. I guess being in charge of six teenagers was bad enough, but being in charge of six teenagers who were about to smuggle Bibles into Communist China was much, much worse. We were told about ten times by Mr. Peterson to be discreet and not to wander far from the hostel (not that our counselor would have let us). I complied and spent most of the next forty-eight hours looking out the hostel's windows at the wondrous city. I think we all were a little disappointed when our contact arrived. I was expecting something like James Bond but instead got a fat and loud Chinese guy. He asked us to walk with him and led the group to a printing house near the hostel. I watched while a press cranked out little green New Testaments in Mandarin and listened as he explained our mission.

Perhaps sensing our edginess, he assured us that even if we got caught, we wouldn't be arrested, as such an action could unnecessarily stir international attention. Instead, we would simply be sent back across the border and prohibited from entering China again; our mission would be over. If we weren't caught, here's what would happen: for the next ten mornings, we would return to the printing press and load as many New Testaments into a metal frame backpack as we could carry. We would each receive train and/or boat tickets to different towns and cities in China, then head out alone. Upon reaching our destination, each of us would walk to a predetermined park near the port or train station. Awaiting us there would be a person on a bench with an identical-looking backpack. We would exchange packs—again, *discreetly*—then lay low for at least six hours before returning to Hong Kong, so as not to alert suspicion at customs. Each evening we'd return to the printing press, drop off our newly emptied backpacks, then retire for the night to our hostel to exchange stories and pray together.

"You'll be perfect," our Hong Kong contact assured us in English as we walked back to the youth hostel. "They will never suspect you all in a million years." The real risk, he explained, was for the Chinese person picking up the Bibles, who might get "prison, or worse." He then took the time to kneel alone with each of us beside our beds and recite a prayer for our safety.

I may have only been fifteen, but I knew that a prayer for safety usually meant something bad could happen. After he left me with a laugh and slap on the back, I assumed the fetal position on my bed and silently cried myself to sleep. I suspect the others did the same.

--- ~~~ ---

On the first day of our new mission, I awoke at dawn a manic mess. I was hearing a cacophony of voices in my head and couldn't focus. I couldn't eat and kept looking behind me. Our host was all business when we arrived at the press. I was given a map and written instructions, tickets, and some last minute advice. He reminded us of the importance of this mission, that the Godless Communists were not allowing the people to read the word of God.

The next few hours can only be described as a dream. Crowded trains. Stern looks at customs. The precious stamp. A man on a bench with an orange backpack. The exchange. A much lighter backpack. Some street-vendor noodles. Bikes everywhere. Markets of foreign vegetables.

I tried—and failed—to enjoy my short days in China and my evenings in Hong Kong. I was too afraid of Communists. Afraid I would be arrested and shot. Afraid of an entire belief system that didn't have room for Jesus. I couldn't speak the language and spent almost every minute in China alone. Manic, I walked and walked, trying to figure out what the hell was going on with my life. By this time, I found my American companions, who complained endlessly, insufferable and spent as little time with them as possible.

My only company, it seemed, was the voice in my head asking the same question over and over again as I manically walked around mainland China. "Chuck? Chuck? Chuck? Chuck?" I steadfastly believed these were not rebukes from God or signs of a mental illness. I knew it, I felt it. I was certain it was a gift. *You should be grateful*, I told myself. But I so wanted those voices to stop.

Chuck?

It was a fair question and I didn't have an answer.

Will the Real Uncle Gunnysack Please Stand Up

I have spoke with the tongue of angels.
I have held the hand of a devil.
It was warm in the night.
I was cold as a stone.

But I still haven't found what I'm looking for.

U2, "I Still Haven't Found What I'm Looking For"

Describing this particular manifestation of my mental illnesses—the hearing of voices—is fairly easy. You hear something in your head that isn't there. And, by and large, society says that's not good. There are exceptions to that rule— the composer who hears music in the shower, the savant muttering advanced equations in his sleep. But for the most part, hearing voices is a no-no. To make them go away, you swallow medications that overwhelm your life. And you get tagged with a fancy disease that is hard to spell. There's nothing good about it, really.

But mania is different. Mania is sexy. Mania is a siren song, in harmony, mainlined right into your veins. You know those days when you wake up full of energy? Clean the house. Finish that term paper early. Bake a cake. Go for a good run. All the while, the ideas are flowing; problems are being creatively solved. It's a damn good feeling. Now multiple that by ten. Add a few cups of coffee and an energy drink to give the high a tremble, and now you are me when I'm manic. And at this point in my life—as a teenager living a WWJD life—I was manic pretty much all the time. I loved it.

Yes, with mania comes the crash. There's always the crash, isn't there? There is the debilitating depression that makes your muscles sad, where just getting yourself to cry is an achievement to be celebrated. But hey, if hangovers stopped drinking, passing prohibition would be a snap. The fact is, it's fun to watch a candle burn from both ends. It's even more fun to be that candle. And I have lit up a lot of rooms. But when I was young, no one was calculating my wax-melt-ratio. No one. I really wish someone had been. That was largely my fault. I never asked for help from my parents or friends, and I hid my down moments from them. And my parents, who were teenagers when they had their first child, didn't know what mental illness looked like, either. For as long as I could remember, they had respected and trusted me enough to give me freedom and independence. I was free to make my own path and my own mistakes. I am not sure they believed what I did: that the voices and the mania were manifestations of a soul on fire, of a young man on a mission for God. But I am sure they believed in me—to a fault.

Of course, I didn't understand any of these things at the time. My experiences in the Philippines and Hong Kong had rattled me, that was for sure, but when I returned home, my fears and uncertainties seemed to melt away, only to be replaced by a new-found conviction that I'd survived some test, that my own version of forty days in the desert had given me further insight into God's will.

During my junior year of high school, I was an insufferable apostle of Christ. I witnessed to schoolmates, inviting them to my house to listen to Petra or Stryper, using Christian rock as an excuse to bring up Jesus. I steered conversations toward Jesus at every family get-together, social gathering, and sporting event. On weekends I would walk door-to-door in my town. My charm and youth often got me inside homes, and there I would tell stories from the Bible, relating them to the plight of unemployment and uncertainty that was plaguing northeastern Ohio. I knew a lot of these folks, or, if not, I was at least one of them. And I wasn't a complete weirdo. I went to prom and was on the football team for a year, playing defensive back, my love of the game being wholly explained by the fact that my position required me to run backward at great speeds. I was poor, but so were most of them. In other words, I fit in. So they listened. And along the way, I convinced many of them to drop to their knees and accept Jesus as their personal Lord and Savior.

No surprise, Missions Outreach Incorporated invited me back the following summer for another round of proselytizing. This time, my help was needed even more. They had a special mission in Haiti, to save souls from Voodoo.

—————

Earlier that year, widespread nonviolent protests across Haiti against the repressive regime of Baby Doc Duvalier had forced the dictator to flee. On February 7, 1986, the U.S. Air Force flew him to exile in France. Much of the nation's riches went with him. A brutal military junta took power. Baby Doc's paramilitary force was known as the Tonton Macoutes, named after the Haitian Creole mythological figure Tonton Macoute, or Uncle Gunnysack, a bogeyman who kidnapped bad children at night in his gunnysack and ate them the next morning for breakfast. Even after Duvalier's exile, its troops prowled the countryside as guns for hire.

Coincidentally, in the same month, the Philippines also had a nonviolent revolution, dubbed the Yellow Revolution because of the yellow ribbons worn by protesters, that ousted a dictator, bringing the twenty-year authoritarian regime of Ferdinand Marcos to an end. As it had done for Baby Doc, the U.S. military aided Marcos's exile. And again, the nation's riches went with him.

Two revolutions in one month: one in a country I'd just left, another in a country where I was headed. I'd watched both events unfold on the nightly news but didn't really understand them or why the United States was involved. When I returned to Missouri for another stint at the MOI, I naturally had a lot of questions. The founder and director of MOI invited me to his house one evening, poured me a glass of sweet tea, and gave me the answers while the cicadas buzzed outside his porch. Both the Marcos and Baby Doc governments were Christian, he explained. Marcos used his power to stop the spread of godless Communism and a heathen Islam. Baby Doc used his to stop the spread of not only Communism but something even worse: Voodoo ("Just a fancy way of saying 'Satan worship'"). The U.S. government, he continued, was uniquely ordained by God with a mandate to save the world. God had anointed President Reagan, too, and if Reagan supported those men, then we should do likewise. Just as Romans 13:1 says, "Let every soul be subject unto higher powers. For there is no power but of God: the powers that be are ordained by God."

Most important, he said, these so-called dictators had allowed Christian missionaries free rein in their respective countries. "We are not in these places to get involved in politics, Chucky. We are there to let the heathens know the everlasting love of Jesus Christ. To compel them to accept Jesus as their personal Lord and Savior. We are there to save souls. Period."

As he spoke, I could see the prostitutes of Olangapo and my old friends, the Guerrillas for God, waving their yellow ribbons with much-deserved defiance and joy. Waving them in the shadows of Clark Air Force Base and Subic Naval Base. Waving them under the disgusted noses of my missionary hosts, the Petersons.

I was being asked to join the "good guys," to accept that Reagan was doing God's work by confronting Communism. But something felt wrong. That night I meditated on the angry Jesus, the one with a whip, the one who drove the moneylenders from the temple. If he was sitting where I was, I wondered what side he would be on. Regardless, I arrived in Haiti in June 1986, ready to save souls.

⸻

My mission team, made up of a small group of male college students and myself, traveled together from MOI headquarters in Bethany, Missouri, to Port-au-Prince. Our new base was in the coastal town of Bainet, at a local church led by former Voodoo practitioners. This church was, by far, the most charismatic I had ever seen. Its goal was to attract other Voodooists susceptible to leaving their trade and then to cast out their demons. Services were held at night, and while church leaders chanted and sang, their penitent guests would froth at the mouth and sweat and speak in the terrible voices of their inner demons. Often they were tied to a cross and beaten. Once the demons were cast out, some would cut large gashes across their arms and chests and thighs with machetes and celebrate by smearing their naked bodies in blood.

I was there to preach, and I did my best. I put on my three-piece suit, prepared sermons, and stood boldly in front of the congregation. But I didn't speak the language and, amid the chaos of the services, I was often left without a translator. I felt my sermons were drowned in the indecipherable cacophony and, honestly, the services were dark and scary to me. I would lay in my hammock afterward, in a hut I shared with my fellow missionaries near the church, with the drums from the service still pounding to the beat of my heart, and slumber off to horrible nightmares.

I spent most of my days with a translator, witnessing house to house. After a couple of weeks, most members of my group left Bainet for a two-day mission. I was asked to stay behind to care for one of our own who had, we later found out, contracted malaria. The man—who must have been no older than twenty-one—adhered to an Evangelical sect that refused medicine of any kind, so he had not been taking his daily doses of quinine. He had been sick for a few days, but just hours after the others left, his condition worsened. My mother once told me that a fever reached its tipping point at 105. Well, there he was at 104. The sweat was actually dripping from the bottom of his hammock.

My memories of Haiti are a little hazy, but I clearly recall one morning when I was carrying a jug of cold water from the local well back to my sick co-missionary. My plan was to cool him with a sponge bath to keep him below the dreaded 105. As I walked back to our camp, I followed behind a loose group of Haitian women carrying water, too, and as I watched their bare feet pad along the dusty ground, I felt I'd fallen into a biblical scene. This was a place where Jesus would boldly come forth and heal. I returned to our hut, set my jug down, and pondered my situation. Here I was, a young man with the discerned gift of the holy spirit of healing, and I hadn't even considered using it. What better time than now? We were alone and he was delirious. No one would know. There was no stage to perform from. Just me, a vessel of God, healing a sick man, maybe saving a life.

But as I stood over his hammock, watching the perspiration bead up, swell, and drip down his face, my doubts set in instead. The group had mentioned that there was a medical missionary team in Jacmel, which was about thirty miles away, just in case we ever needed it. With that in mind, I bent down, kissed his fire-hot cheek, and whispered in his ear that he'd be fine. I was going to get help.

—*mm*—

I'd been told a journey of thirty miles to Jacmel could take five or six hours or more. But off I went, a sixteen-year-old American, just months after a revolution, in search of a doctor. Thankfully, the bus trip—a bumpy thrill ride—took less than two hours. The medics I met in Jacmel naturally weren't thrilled about releasing a staff person for possibly two days to treat an American who refused to take medicine. But they did it—another miracle?—sending me back to Bainet with a young American nurse from Pennsylvania.

The return trip was slow. The bus driver was a fan of long cigarette breaks, the engine suffered some clattering malfunction, an obstinate herd of goats blocked a winding road. It would be many, many hours before we arrived in the pitch black to a delirious man.

During that long hot trip, the nurse and I talked. She was a Mennonite, and she patiently answered my questions about her people and what they believed. She told me about pacifism, something I had never heard of before. She didn't call herself a missionary. She didn't believe in proselytizing or setting up churches. And when I heard about how many lives she had saved—literally saved through her medical work—my bouts of faith healing seemed more than a little silly. We both believed in the same Jesus and were both there in Haiti to do his work. Yet the nature of our work couldn't have been more different. She asked if I was considering college. I told her I was applying to Moody Bible Institute and Pensacola Christian College but that my first choice was Liberty Baptist University because I admired Jerry Falwell so much. She told me she recently graduated from a Christian college, too. A Mennonite school called Goshen College. I promised her I would look into it when I got back home.

During our ride, the recent revolution also came up. I regurgitated to her what I had been told about God's plan here, about Reagan's divine mandate to quell Communism. After my diatribe, with all the love and kindness she could muster, she reached over to hold my hands, looked into my eyes and told me "the truth." The truth was that some men of God do not have Jesus in their hearts and that these men burnish God like a weapon for money and power. She explained that since time untold religion has been used to enslave, conquer, and destroy. She said that such men can transform the most beautiful things into the most hideous. Her words resonated with a lot of what I had seen and experienced in the last few years. "What would Jesus do?" That's the question she said I should use as my litmus test.

"Don't forget," she added. "You know God, too."

—*m*—

Thanks mostly to the nurse and the meds that the man finally agreed to swallow—and not my divine gifts—his fever broke; his life was spared. But meanwhile, cracks in the wall of my belief system were beginning to form. My concerns at first were not so much theological but political. My mentors' easy answers explaining away the revolutions in the Philippines and Haiti weren't sitting well. And that young nurse from Haiti, I couldn't get her out of my mind—her love and her logic kept echoing inside me. I had now seen both countries with my own eyes, and it was obvious that their repressive leaders were not very Christian and that the revolutions seemed, well, *reasonable*. There was systemic poverty on a scale that demanded immediate action. What would Jesus do, indeed?

—*mm*—

The old man in the Olds '88 took his cock out while I was looking out the window at the Utah desert and asked me to kiss it.

The advice my older brother had given me weeks earlier now came in handy. When hitchhiking, he told me, always carry a knife and bring plenty of water.

I took a deep breath, calmly slid my knife from the front pocket of my backpack, and told the old man to pull over. He sighed and did as I asked, depositing me on the side of the road in the oppressive summer heat. I put my knife away, walked to the nearest overpass of glorious shade, took a long drink from my two-gallon Coleman water jug, arranged my bag to make a pillow, and settled down on a concrete slab.

I was now eighteen years old and, thanks to the advice of that nurse in Haiti, I had applied for and already accepted a scholarship to Goshen College, which is not far from South Bend, Indiana. It was June 1987; high school was over. My brother and sister were both in the military, and I was the last kid at home, so my parents—who, in their mid-forties, were still relatively young— seized at a chance for a great adventure and moved to Alaska. I was excited for them. Before they left, my dad got me a summer job at a local ladder factory. The plan was to stay at my parents' place rent free until college and save up money for school. But after two weeks of fastening the same two rivets on the upper left rung of hundreds of step ladders, I'd had enough. My parents were gone and I soon would be, too. Screw this job. Screw this town. Screw the poverty and despair of the Rust Belt. I'll take freedom over money. I was, after all, my father's son.

So without a party or any goodbyes I decided right then and there, with only the cash I'd earned in two weeks at the factory, to put my thumb out the next day in front of my house and, alone, hitchhike from Ohio to San Francisco. In the fall, I'd hitchhike directly back to Goshen.

Many years later, I realize what a big decision that was. I never again lived in Ohio. I didn't write. I didn't keep up. I didn't visit. When I go back now, for the occasional funeral, I feel like I am entering a foreign yet familiar land. I sincerely regret the bridges I burned by not saying goodbye, by not keeping in touch. But every time I go "home" now I am counting the hours to when I can leave again. At the time I left, I didn't realize it, but I was becoming a brand-new person. There are many ways to be born again.

I also think I left because I just wanted to be anonymous for a while, to think in solitude about my personal relationship with Jesus, about where that relationship had taken me over the previous two years. I wanted a break from *doing* things for God and to focus on loving the actual God. And there was something else: the voices in my head were becoming more frequent. I felt a need to confront them anew. Were they angels, as I had been told by Preacher Randy, Mr. Peterson, and others I looked up to in the church? Was God talking with me, guiding me? Or was I mentally ill? The fact was that I had grown scared of them. They were not in my control, and as their gibberish had turned into single words that were now beginning to form sentences, I feared they were going to start telling me to do things I didn't want to do.

But it wasn't just the voices in my head or Jesus that traveled with me as I hitchhiked to San Francisco. I had political questions to mull over as well. Was the Lord really against the revolutions in the Philippines and Haiti? Was Ronald Reagan anointed by God? What were missionaries really doing to solve the problems in their host countries? Was salvation enough? What about bread or clean water? What if they were on the wrong side?

Maybe that's why I picked as my destination San Francisco, a city I pictured as America's own little hotbed of revolution.

Feeling pretty badass after surviving numerous sexual advances, cold nights under bridges, and a gambling-addicted long hauler who considered me his good luck charm, I arrived in the city with $350 in my pocket and no friends. Before I checked out the Golden Gate Bridge or the trolley cars or the corner of Haight-Ashbury, however, I visited a tattoo parlor.

I considered imprinting the crucified Jesus on my upper left shoulder, but it was out of my price range. I pondered a number of other Christian icons (like the ichthys "Jesus fish") but then turned to my hitchhiking journal. On the inside cover I found it—my own sketch of an orange smiley-faced sun, wearing sunglasses and breaking through fluffy pink clouds, a flock of tiny m-shaped birds in the distance. A pierced and tattoo-covered man injected the ink into my skin. I wore a muscle shirt for days as I wandered through Fisherman's Wharf and the Mission District, imagining that my tender shoulder now bore the symbol of the world's most hard-core scalawag.

After a week of sleeping on park benches and beaches I was tired and cold. And a little bored. My vague plan of spending some "quality time" alone with Jesus was upended by the discovery that I actually wanted something to *do* for the rest of the summer. And then I met a woman named Grace. During a break as she canvassed for the National Abortion Rights Action League, or NARAL, she sat down at a table next to me in a coffee shop. Seeing her clipboard and assorted papers, I asked her what she was up to. She handed me a flyer. The word "abortion" leaped from the page. I was appalled. She was raising money for baby killers, and that's basically what I accused her of, loudly, ignoring the glares from neighboring tables. Grace apparently had experience arguing with right-wingers because she gave it right back. After some back and forth, it seemed we'd reached an impasse. But then she did something peculiar. She asked if she could show me something.

"Sure, why not?" Like I said, I was bored and game for anything.

We got in her car and drove to a Catholic church in Oakland.

The church was active in the sanctuary movement. Sanctuary, Grace explained, created an underground railroad of sorts between like-minded churches—mostly Catholic, Quaker, and Mennonite (my Goshen antennae perked up here)—that moved victims of the U.S.-backed wars in Central America into sympathetic communities in America and Canada. At the moment, the church was hosting approximately forty refugees from Nicaragua, who, having fled the U.S.-backed Contras, were living in its basement. Grace led me down the stairs into a corridor that branched into several rooms usually reserved for Sunday school classes. As we walked, I was reminded of Olongapo and Bainet. Throughout the little network of rooms, women were folding clothes or preparing meals, and children were running around in colorful clothing. Somber men were chatting in small groups. And there was singing. It was the spontaneous singing that took me aback. When do the rest of us ever break out into song?

In some of the rooms, cots were filled with decaying canvas bags bulging with a life's worth of belongings. I could only imagine the stress the refugees must be experiencing and how exhausted they must be, not to mention the hell of their not-so-distant past and the uncertainty ahead.

Our tour left me wanting to know more, so I asked Grace to introduce me to one of the nuns. I asked if I could stay and help out for a few days. For about a week I slept on the basement floor with the refugees and volunteered to do dishes and cook and clean and move boxes and run errands. I listened, too. I knew some basic Spanish, but Grace, who was fluent, helped translate as I got to know my new roommates. Together, they patiently explained to me about death squads and the Contras and the mothers of the disappeared.

My inner voices occasionally drove me out of the basement to church upstairs, where I would spend time praying alone. As I was kneeling in a pew one morning, a nun approached me and struck up a conversation. Over the next few days, we took several afternoon walks together. I talked her ear off and asked a million questions. Eventually she lent me a book that truly and forever changed my life: *The Gospel in Solentiname* by Ernesto Cardenal.

Cardenal was a member of the Nicaraguan Sandinistas that the Reagan-backed Contras were fighting against, and he was also Nicaragua's minister of culture from 1979 to 1987. Not only was he a Marxist, he was the poet patron saint of a belief system and movement within Roman Catholicism that interpreted the teachings of Christ through the eyes of the poor. It was called liberation theology. It was the foundation of the sanctuary movement. And it was the antithesis of so much that I'd been taught.

The whole experience took my breath away. I mean that. I kind of breathed it all in, and I don't think I've ever quite exhaled. I was reminded again of the Mennonite nurse from Jacmel, of the feelings she stirred in me. She'd be worthy of this place. A true Christian. Not like me.

As I read and spent time with the nuns and refugees and Grace, I could almost hear the cracks in my faith turning into fissures. I remember studying Joshua at the time and thinking about his faithful band of trumpeters bringing down the walls of Jericho. "That's what I need," I thought. "I need some walls tumblin' down."

During the rest of that summer, I witnessed to no one. I told no one of my gift of the Spirit or my work as a missionary. Through Grace, I met a lot of other young, liberal Christians. We would hike in the Redwood Forest, listen to free concerts in the park and talk for hours. Gradually, I began to feel that I'd been practicing the mean-spirited version of our shared faith. And as I thought more deeply about my experiences as a missionary, I started to feel shame and, worse, anger. The sanctuary refugees, the Mennonite nurse, the nuns and Grace and her friends: there was no denying their service and love for Jesus. But I wasn't them. I was someone else entirely. It was like there were two Jesuses, two Gods, two Holy Spirits existing in parallel universes. And there I was, a leg now planted firmly in both.

A Crack in an Open Door

We go to the Bible, we go through the workout.
We read up on revival and we stand up for the
    lookout.
There's more than one answer to these questions,
pointing me in a crooked line
The less I seek my source for some definitive
The closer I am to fine.

Indigo Girls, "Closer I Am to Fine"

Mennonites have this strange little pastime they call the Mennonite Name Game. Here's how it starts:
"Hi, I'm Carl Yoder from Lancaster County."
"I'm Eliza Swartzendruber from Elkhart County. Good to meet you!"
With eager smiles and inexhaustible stamina, my peers at Goshen College would then launch into the all-important task of tracing through their lineages in order to discover what relatives—alive or dead—they had in common. If, after unlimited tries, you still couldn't determine whether you were sixth cousins twice removed, then you sighed and moved on to the consolation round of Naming All the People You Both Knew in Common, which tended to be numerous. The Friesens, Kauffmans, Garbers, Geingrichs, Millers, and Lapps at Goshen played this game every time they met someone new. My freshman orientation felt like a genealogy class. Inevitably, this would happen:
"Hi, I'm Bethany Schmucker from Lancaster County."

"Hi, I'm Chuck Kane from all over the place but mostly Ohio. Good to meet you!"

Silence. A smile.

Don't get me wrong, I loved Goshen and thought Mennonites were the coolest Christians, just as my nurse companion in Haiti had said they would be. They were pacifists, politically left leaning, environmentally conscious, and they had great potlucks after church. But for an outsider, a nonethnic Mennonite, the social structure was tricky to maneuver, even exclusionary at times. Students cooked using recipes from the Mennonite cookbook *More with Less*. They traveled the country using the directory *Mennonite Your Way*, a book that connected you to other Mennonites who would allow you to sleep in their extra room and who would presumably play the Name Game with you.

I remember being startled at my first Maple Leaf soccer match, when the student section burst out singing the doxology at 6:06 p.m. You see, "606" was the page number on which "Praise God from Whom All Blessings Flow" appeared in their hymnal (in 1992, it was moved to page 118—the horror!). The students loved this song, and they sang with such power and beauty—always a cappella and in four-part harmony, per tradition—that I admired them. But I also remember one morning at chapel, when a student next to me politely suggested I might just lip synch the words, the implication being that I was marring the harmony for everyone else. I felt a twinge of alienation then, a little reminder that I wasn't one of them.

Mennonites also had other issues I struggled with, including their long-held ban on dancing. There's an old joke: "Q: Why can't Mennonites have sex? A: It might lead to dancing." Coincidentally, my freshman year marked the first time that Goshen students would be allowed to dance. Boy, was everyone excited! This might have been a minor footnote in my life except for how events unfolded during the first official on-campus dance.

About halfway through my senior year in high school, I'd decided to break off a three-year relationship with my girlfriend, Shannon. Shannon and I had been active together in Southington Life's youth group and, in keeping with our strict moral codes, we were careful to never cross any inappropriate sexual lines. We hung out on second base for hours in the back of her dad's car, watched a lot of VHS tapes, and talked of traveling the world. I was madly in love with her (as only a sixteen-year-old can be), but, knowing that I'd be attending Goshen and she'd be going to Ohio State, I broke up with her, blaming geography. Shannon was the intense, possessive type and our breakup was a protracted and dramatic affair. But by the time I got to Goshen, having finished high school and having spent the summer in San Francisco, I'd moved on. Presumably, so had she. At that first dance, however, there she was, standing on the newly christened dance floor. It was the first time I'd seen her since I'd left Ohio, and she was beautiful as ever.

To my great surprise, Shannon informed me that she had enrolled in Goshen. Beaming, she told me she had missed freshman orientation and the first week of classes, but she was here now, a non-Mennonite undergrad, just like me!

I didn't know what to say, but inwardly, I was not thrilled. Because Goshen is a very small school, I knew Shannon's presence would change everything. I would see her everywhere. I didn't want that. I wanted to be on my own, to be somewhere where no one knew my past, to reinvent myself. As we continued our awkward chatting over the loud music I felt the overwhelming urge to flee. So I did. When she excused herself to go to the bathroom, I snuck away to the student union to watch MTV. At the time, Guns N' Roses' "Welcome to the Jungle" video had just come out and was on almost all the time. My plan was to see how many times I could watch it in two hours, alone, away from the dance and with space to consider how my ex-girlfriend might shake up my new life.

Of course, being on my own at Goshen meant that I was also extremely lonely. And after an hour or so, when Shannon eventually found me in the union (such a small school!) and sat next to me on the couch, I have to admit I welcomed her company and familiar face. We talked for a while, but every conversation petered out, ending in silence or awkward laughs during another viewing of "Welcome to the Jungle."

Then Shannon flipped the script.

"Want to play pool?" she asked. "If you beat me you can eat me."

This was an inside joke of ours. Shannon was a serious baker and cook, and often, when we had played darts or a game of pool or whatever, she would hold up a plate of homemade cookies or egg rolls and deliver the same line. But this time she had no food.

I agreed to play. I won the game. She may have let me win.

Because everyone was at the dance, it was no problem sneaking back to her dorm room. The rules at Goshen allowed boys and girls to be in each other's rooms at preset times, but the door had to be open. *How* open, of course, was a point of great contention on campus—just a crack in the door? Halfway? But that didn't matter now. We shut the door and turned the lock.

I remember two things very clearly.

One, we both went straight for intercourse. No kissing. No fondling. Nothing but intercourse. After all those discussions in high school about which sexual touching was acceptable in God's eyes, after hours of prayer and blurred lines for some three years, I lost my virginity quickly and without a moment's thought. We just walked in her dorm, took off our pants, and did it.

The second thing I remember was her breasts. Yes, she had beautiful breasts, and I'd spent many hours touching and kissing them in high school. But now, just when I was about to enter her and was fumbling with the buttons on her shirt, she flatly told me I couldn't see them or touch them. She was engaged to a boy back home, she said, an older guy, and those breasts were for him because he liked them so much.

"But tonight my vagina is for you."

What did that even *mean*?

Like any good first time, I came in about one minute, pulling out seconds early so I could ejaculate on my rolled up undies. I repeated this four more times in less than ten minutes. We didn't use protection, and after our final congress, Shannon's mood suddenly, and violently, turned. She began punching a nearby pillow over and over again, and then she started yelling, at no one or nothing in particular. In a daze, I put on my pants, grabbed my very soiled underwear, and left without a word. I could feel my old loathing of sin and guilt welling up in me. I sprinted from her dorm to the chapel, the thumping bass of the Mennonites' first dance echoing across the grassy lawns, and ran to the altar, where I got on my knees and cried my eyes out, vowing to God that I would never ever do *that* again until I was married.

The shame of lustful memories would haunt me for weeks. I prayed and prayed, but I also masturbated while thinking about sex with Shannon. At times, I saw myself as the character in the "Welcome to the Jungle" video who got off the bus as a pure young man but ended up tainted by the world. I was no longer pure and would have to admit that to my future wife. I hated myself for it.

I might have talked about all of this with Shannon. But the day after we had sex, when I went to see her, hoping to make sense of what had happened and maybe apologize in some awkward way, I found she was gone.

"She left," her dorm mate told me.

As in, she had moved out. Shannon was out of the dorm, and out of Goshen College. Moved in on a Friday and was gone by Saturday. Surprisingly, I never saw or heard from her again.

—◆—

As time passes and hearts mend and young men smell flowers, they fall in love again, and so it was for me. Erma was her name. She was very Mennonite—sweet and intelligent and chaste—and she exuded a normalcy and stability I craved. I just wanted to play cards with her, kiss a little bit, study a lot, and have a pretty girl to hang out with. Was that asking too much?

But by my second trimester at school, I was in trouble. Goshen may have been a laid-back liberal arts school in Indiana, but I was feeling academic and social pressure. I was proud to be the first Kane to go to college, but my quaint little high school had left me ill prepared for the academic rigors of a private college. Being a non-Mennonite certainly didn't help. But the real problem was my mental illness.

The voices in my head had not stayed in Ohio. To the contrary, responding perhaps to the stress I was under, they intruded almost daily. I was so manic at times that I would literally hyperventilate. The only way I could sleep was to take long naps when my roommate was gone so I could cry myself to sleep. My assigned roommate, Keith Miller, was a white African who rarely spoke to anyone. He may have been the shyest person I had ever met. How we got hooked up as dorm mates was beyond me. Born in Tanzania and raised in Kenya by Mennonite missionaries, this was his first time in the United States. He, too, was struggling with culture shock. He coped by retreating into solitary endeavors like reading and art. When we were together, I would talk to him for hours while he read. I would make shit up, blatant lies, because I just needed to talk, to make sounds to mask the voices, to release the air out of my balloon. I developed new tics, nervously clearing my throat almost constantly and unconsciously touching my nose. I couldn't stop. Keith must have found me to be the most annoying roommate ever. But I knew I was falling apart—the Herculean effort to keep it all together was not working.

One day Erma, bless her heart, was giving me a haircut in the commons room of her dorm. She was clipping away at the frayed ends of my ponytail when she asked me to look up so she could adjust the angle of a cut. As I did so, I noticed a cabinet door on the other side of the room was slightly ajar. It was dark inside, and I was suddenly filled with the need to be in there. It appeared to me as a sort of panic room, a place to hide from the forces bearing down on my mind. So I calmly got up, walked to the cabinet, swept away everything from inside it, and crawled in. I remember very little after that, except that a few days later, a nurse asked me if I knew where I was. I shook my head no. She told me I was in the Oaklawn Psychiatric Center.

I looked around and remember being kind of disappointed. No straight jackets. No locked doors. No bars on the windows. This place did not look like the loony bin at all. I even had my street clothes on. But my disappointment soon dissolved when I looked down at my laceless sneakers and realized I was rocking back and forth. I should have been horrified at my situation. But the drugs had numbed that.

At the time, being institutionalized was the best thing for me. I was a definite flight risk, even though I knew damn well I had nowhere to go. Being locked up and cared for was just what I needed. My mind was frail, and I struggled to discern what was real from what was not. That struggle was exhausting, but I also recognized it was dangerous. Any delusions of grandeur of being a faith healer were gone, as were the illusions that my voices were angels or that I was a prophet receiving messages from God. And I'd been lying to myself. My academic struggles at Goshen shattered my internal myth that I was some sort of genius. Instead, these were the facts. I had a manic disorder. I had schizophrenia. (Schizophrenia, though, proved many years later to be a misdiagnosis, as doctors subsequently labeled me with bipolar 1 disorder.) In the weeks after that initial diagnosis, all of the one-on-one therapy, the reading materials, the group sessions, and the meds combined to yield a revelation—I was not falling apart; I was disassociating from reality.

I was mentally ill, and I had to accept it.

But I wouldn't accept that my life was over. My parents were in Alaska, and I opted not to tell them right away. My rationale was that this was *my* fight. After about a month at Oaklawn, I went the out-patient route and returned to school during the day. I took my lithium and thorazine. I busted my ass in class (and got all As and Bs my second trimester). I joined the cross-country team (steeplechase). I went to therapy every day. I prayed a lot, asking God to help me put one foot in front of the other—nothing more. I went to chapel to worship, my clearer head helping me just enjoy Jesus's love. I grew my hair until my ponytail stretched down my back. I pierced my ear. I experimented in making art. I thoroughly delighted in all that college life had to offer. And not once did I get confused about what was real or get so manic that my jaw would ache the next day from grinding my teeth. The voices had disappeared. That feeling in my chest that at any second I could implode likewise was gone. If this was normal, I liked it.

—␣␣—

My summer break after my freshman year left me with some choices. My parents had made their trip to Alaska official and now lived on a remote island in Prince William Sound. My sister lived in Anchorage on a military base and my brother was a long hauler. I could stay in Goshen, get an apartment, and compete with other college students for a crappy job. Or I could take a risk with the rest of the money I had, travel to Alaska, and make my fortune as a commercial fisherman. I chose the latter. My sister's home became my home base. From there I found my summer job: for a little more than three months, I worked for Icicle Seafood in Seward.

My first job was in the hull of a long-liner, categorizing black cod as they flew down a belt at me and a few other guys. We'd divide them by weight grouping (between four and nine pounds), tossing them two at a time onto frozen metal pallets in the hull of the boat. It was backbreaking work. Salmon season came next, when we used nets instead of longlines to haul in huge piles of beautiful fish. I was a tech, meaning I was in charge of dividing the silvers and sockeyes and chums and pinks. My favorite jobs came during the brief but fruitful halibut seasons: three twenty-four-hour windows randomly determined by wildlife officials only a few days in advance. In those frenzied, daylong sprees, I was in charge of guillotining the massive fish (some weighed up to four hundred pounds). All of the work was tough and smelly and, at times, it was dangerous, but in the course of three months I made more than $15,000. Coupled with my scholarship, I now had enough cash to never work again while I was at Goshen.

Not having to work meant that over the next few years, I was able to take unpaid Christian volunteer jobs in different parts of the country. The most memorable was a summer job after my sophomore year at the Hospitality Community in Georgia.

Fashioned after the Catholic Worker movement (founded by one of my Christian heroes, Dorothy Day), Hospitality advocated for and ministered to death-row inmates and the local homeless population. Their theology was similar to that of the nuns in Oakland. Everything they offered—meals, free showers, shelter, shoes, and clothes—they offered with dignity. *That*, I realized, was truly radical.

I worked the breakfast shift. Many of our "friends on the streets," as we called them, worked as temporary day laborers. Paid minimum wage or less, they logged twelve- to sixteen-hour days doing demeaning and often dangerous work with few if any breaks. They had no rights, no benefits, yet they would line up as early as 5 a.m., waiting for trucks to drive by and pick them up for a day's work. Our job was to greet them in line with a twenty-four-ounce Styrofoam cup filled with hot cheese grits and two shelled hard-boiled eggs on top. Another twenty-four-ounce cup had sweet milky coffee. A plastic baggie held two peanut butter and honey sandwiches for lunch.

During my summer there, I became friends with a man named Bob. He was a homeless man right out of central casting. An alcoholic and a vet, Bob was old and grew his white beard long. His fingers and mustache were stained from the roll-your-own Bugler tobacco he smoked. One day shortly after I met him, Bob told me that he had pretty much decided to give up, to die. He was stoic, like the men in my family, so I knew he meant what he said. His plan was to find a cozy spot under some kudzu and drink himself to death.

Bob, whether he knew it or not, became a screen onto which my nineteen-year-old self projected a hundred different notions. Sure, I saw a human being who needed help, but I also saw Jesus. "Who is Jesus?" Surprisingly, this was the first time I was really asking myself this cornerstone theological question. Was Jesus a refugee from Nicaragua? A prostitute in the Philippines? And what about me? Was Jesus me, too? What about the homeless alcoholic in Georgia? And why was Bob even on the streets in the first place? In Bob I saw the latent functions of the social and economic policies of Ronald Reagan. In Bob I saw America, the land of the free and the home of the brave, kicking its neediest to the curb and then kicking them in the teeth for good measure. My growing disdain for capitalism solidified in the face of Bob. How could I not want to overthrow the system? How could I not want a revolution?

But I saw something else in Bob, too. I saw me at his age, drunk and vulnerable on the streets, hearing voices and talking to myself. I saw me needing help but being too proud or confused to ask for it. I saw me making the decision to kill myself. I saw myself hiding under my parents' bed with my hands over my ears, trying to make the sounds stop. I saw that little crack in the cabinet door, that prison I mistook for a panic room. I thought I knew what he was going through, and I knew it fucking sucked. But I damn well wasn't going to let him drink himself to death. I wasn't going to let us die.

—————

Meanwhile, there was Samantha. A chubby middle-aged southern belle type who volunteered at the Hospitality Community, she was a leader at her local Presbyterian church. She was also the pastor's wife. While stirring grits together late one night at Hospitality to prepare for our day labor ministry, I told her about my routine of jogging at sundown each day. My route, it turns out, ran through her neighborhood. As she added shredded cheese to a big vat of grits, she said, "If you ever get parched in this southern heat, just knock." And she gave me her address.

I jogged by Samantha's house about four times before I had enough guts to stop and knock. Hey, I was thirsty.

Samantha invited me in with a smile. I was a very intense young man, and we quickly were talking about politics and theology. As we chatted on her couch and sipped sweet tea in the air conditioning, she commented on how I was likely getting chilled in my sweat soaked running clothes. She offered to draw me a bath, marking perhaps the first time that I had heard the words "draw" and "bath" in the same sentence. Speechless, I followed her to the tub.

Any lingering questions about her intent disappeared as she took off my clothes, slowly, and put me in the bath. She then soaped up her hands and washed me. Every time she would stroke my cock I would moan out. And every time I was about to cum she would stop. I left her house confused and painfully frustrated, yes, but it was a sweet agony. One I was already anticipating on my jog tomorrow.

<center>~~~</center>

For a few days, I couldn't find Bob. I spent hours looking for him, and when I finally found him he was in sorry shape—open sores, hair falling out—and he was angry. We talked for hours, but he was not willing to come to Hospitality for a meal and a shower and a bit of detox. I didn't ask him to stop drinking or anything, just not to kill himself right now. I asked for and received a lot of great advice from the more seasoned members of Hospitality about what to say and what to offer. But in the end I just sat under the kudzu vines in the nasty hovel Bob called his grave, among his feces and the 20/20 Mad Dog bottles, and proceeded to get ripped myself. I got Bob cups of crushed ice from the nearby 7-Eleven, and we toasted to my first drink of alcohol. A little tipsy, I told him my story. Not the one about the mental institution or my mission-ary work. I told him about moving all the time when I was a kid, about the eccentric men in my family and how much I admired them. About listening to my parents fight about money. I told him about fishing in Canada for an entire summer with my family. An entire summer fishing with your old man? Imagine that! All those rich kids at Goshen who had better table manners and fancy books on their shelves growing up never had that, did they? I proceeded to get more and more angry and drunk, as I took the working-class chip off my shoulder and held it high, railing against God knows what.

Bob clapped a few times and shook his head a lot. He tried to get up, but he fell, too drunk to walk. He then started talking to himself, lost in his own world. Acting on instinct, I kneeled in front on him and put my hand on his forehead. I prayed for God to heal him. I prayed and I prayed and I cried out, asking that if I ever had this gift, may it work right now. *Please God, just one more time. Please!*

Bob lived. I would see him from time to time at the soup kitchen or on the streets. We would sometimes chat, but we never talked like we did that day again. Seeing him alive always made me breathe easy. I am not sure why. Part of it, I am sure, was that I was an arrogant teenager who thought he'd saved someone. But later I also realized that there was a part of Bob I had romanticized—his addiction, his giving into alcohol so openly, so publicly, was beautiful to me. Being an addict and surviving it, without compromise, was sticking it to the man in a way that none of the men of my family ever pulled off. The fact was, I admired it.

Years later, when I was living in Eastern Europe, I did a lot of meth. I did it for fun—so I could talk, dance, escape, and be fucked up. But I considered being addicted to it, too. I romanticized the choice in my mind—the decision of whether to give myself to meth's intense calling, to see where it would take me. To truly skate the edge. And, like Bob, to give a great big "fuck you" to this game of life we all had inherited.

I continued my blue-ball jogging excursions to Samantha's house a few days a week. Things had progressed to her being naked as well, but the rules were clear. I could not touch her, she could only touch me. And she did, often for an hour or more. Sometimes I would cum on my run home as my jogging shorts ever so lightly rubbed against my throbbing penis.

One day while stirring grits, she informed me of the end game. I was not to masturbate for the next week (I was nineteen, so that was an eternity), and then I would come to her home and we would have sex. It had been more than a year since I lost my virginity, and I certainly had not changed my mind about that one slipup being my last until I was married. But damn, did I want to have sex with this woman. Bad.

If I told you I prayed about this predicament, I would be lying. From the moment Samantha asked me, I had every intention of going to her house in a week. I had no idea what particular sex games she had in mind, but I knew I was going to like it. By the third day I couldn't sleep and was irritable. By the morning of day five I was nearly insane. On the agreed-upon night, my jog to her house was more of a sprint. She greeted me at the door in a negligee, the first time I had ever seen one on a real person. She must have felt satisfied when my jaw hit the floor. She took me by the hand to her master bedroom, and we started to kiss, which I realized was our first. She let me touch her all over and I was losing control. She loved it as she reined me in over and over again. As I was about to reach a climax I couldn't control, she stopped me again and had me chill on the bed. "Relax. I don't want you to cum that way. I want to feel you cum inside me." And then she kissed me with what can only be described as intent. When she excused herself to go to the adjacent bathroom, I tried to get my hard-on under control.

I must have heard the voice first, based on the geography of the space.

"Honey, I'm home!"

The look on Samantha's face as she darted from the bathroom surely must have been priceless. I don't remember it though. All I remember was fear. I was not very wise in the world of sex but I knew a jealous husband meant serious business. At what point he saw my jogging clothes and shoes lying on his living room floor doesn't really matter, because Samantha had me out that first-story window in seconds flat. By grace, a pair of his boxer shorts came raining down soon after on the bush that I had fallen through. I was scraped up and bloody, my perfectly good erection ruined.

—*mm*—

The next morning may be ranked among the worst of my life. The couple that started and ran the Hospitality Community wanted to speak with me alone. On the coffee table between us were the jogging clothes and shoes I'd left behind at Samantha's, now laundered and neatly folded.

They didn't talk to me about Jesus or even morality. The congregation at Samantha's church, they explained, were not only major donors to the Hospitality Community; they formed the group's volunteering core. Samantha's husband, the pastor, was on the board of directors. My lack of foresight and the potential consequences of my actions, they told me, could cost Hospitality volunteers and funding for its new temporary day labor breakfast ministry. My indiscretion could come at a price to the homeless.

"This isn't about your sin, Chuck," the director said to me. "That's between you and God. This is about your actions having a negative impact on our work."

I knew, after only one month there, that they were going to ask me to leave. Why would they keep me around? I only had another six weeks left anyway. I repeated my apologies and told them I would do whatever is best for the community. If they needed me to leave, I would leave. Surprisingly, they asked me to stay.

At that moment, I knew what it meant to feel broken. It didn't even occur to me to blame Samantha for her role. I had chosen sin, and the weight of it was pressing on my chest. But those two ministers—whose service to the homeless and to the death-row inmates of Georgia was beyond repute—forgave me. No stipulations. No double-secret probations. No penance. No guilt. Just healing. Just grace.

Flying Too Close to the Sun

How long to sing this song.
How long to sing this song.
How long . . . how long . . . how long . . .
How long . . . to sing this song.

U2, "40"

Six months after I left the Hospitality Community, and with another trimester down at Goshen College, a bus dropped me off alone in Guaitil, a dusty desert town in Costa Rica's northwestern province of Guanacaste. The people of Guaitil are known, if they are known at all, for keeping up the five-thousand-year-old tradition of making Chorotega indigenous pottery. Without electricity or running water this village creates a stunning variety of pottery using the same techniques and, as some claim, the same tools as their ancestors who emigrated there.

I was in Costa Rica for my study service trimester, or SST, a Goshen-required international stint that could have sent me to East Berlin or Martinique or China. I chose Costa Rica. Working in a village that specialized in an ancient craft was simply too romantic for me to pass up. My job would be to teach English at the local elementary school, learn Spanish, and make some pottery on the side.

Not long after I arrived, however, I learned that the elementary school had just started its three-month summer break. My host grandmother spoke mostly Chorotegan, and her stepdaughter, who became my pottery mentor, hardly spoke to anyone at all. So, if I wanted to spend a trimester sitting alone, quietly making pottery in 110-degree heat all day, I was in luck. Although it was in fact the last thing I wanted to do—given that ever since my days of self-inflicted nosebleeds at bedtime, solitude and I had not made a good mix—it seemed that at least for a while, I was going to be making pottery in virtual silence.

We made the pottery in a thatched open-air porch right next to the house. My host grandmother's stepdaughter, who lived next door, was an expert potter. She walked me through every step, every detail, from where to acquire the raw ingredients of mud and minerals to make our pots to how to properly polish the finished products with burnishing stones that had been passed down for hundreds if not thousands of years.

The few times she spoke to me, her words were always presented as gravely important. She would chastise me when I inevitably strayed from her instructions and tried to make my own art.

"Carlos, art is for the leisure class. We are campesinos. This is work."

She took such pride in being a craftsman. Art, to her, was a waste of time and resources.

—*www*—

Almost all of the potters in the village were women because most of the men worked more than half the year in the banana plantations along the Limonese coast of Costa Rica, more than a day's journey from the village. Because of this, the porch was a busy place. On any given evening, a call might come in from a man trying to reach his sister, wife, children, or mother, and the village would stop and gather around the porch. The recipient of the phone call would be given some space for privacy, but once she hung up, everyone wanted to immediately chitchat about it. The women seemed to live for those calls.

The other diversion from pottery was a monthly weekend trip to the coast. You always knew it was coming because the old men of the village started making *guaro*, a fermented palm oil. They would start felling trees about three days in advance. After lopping off the tops and bottoms of the trees they would stuff the ends of the trunks with palm leaves. As the days went by the palm sap became more and more alcoholic. Or as the villagers put it, it became "all *guaro*." Around Thursday afternoon, a man would show up with a pig to roast, two buses and many cases of cola. The women of the village spent Friday mornings making stacks of tortillas, roasting coffee beans, and preparing salsas.

Everyone packed their own hammocks, and we jammed our gear into the buses and headed to the Pacific Ocean for the weekend-long fiesta, where we'd sleep in the open air and, when hungry, rip meat off the pig with a tortilla or grab a ripe mango from a nearby tree. Everyone swam and talked and drank *guaro* and Coke with lime. I decided that *guaro* and Coke with lime had to be better than Mad Dog 20/20 with Bob. I was very correct.

I attended several of these trips, but I remember one well. I was chilling out on the sand, just looking at the ocean and enjoying only the second alcoholic drink of my life, when I thought about the fact that it happened to be a Sunday, the Lord's day, and that I hadn't been to church since arriving here. Come to think of it, no one had. The town had no church, and my abuela's home didn't feature the crosses or religious candles or even Bibles that I thought were commonplace in Latin America. There were no blessings or "Marias." These people, I supposed, were likely Catholic but just very private about it. But maybe they weren't. Maybe they were pagan. Or atheist.

———*ww*———

I set my drink down and headed to a small grove of palm trees in the distance. There, in private, I decided I was going to have church. I first bathed in the ocean, focusing on the memories of my baptism. I got some Bible verses ready in my head and walked to the clearing between the trees. I got down on my knees and prayed. I didn't have anything to ask for or even any concerns so I prayed out of love. It was pure worship. But for the first time since the day of my salvation I did not feel the presence of God. I felt nothing. I didn't weep or get angry. But there it was: the absence of God.

This was certainly a pivotal moment in my life, and I didn't even make the decision—I felt like God did. Still to this day, I'm not sure what happened. Why did I feel the presence of God leave? I didn't want it to happen. Despite my misgivings about how religion could be misused, I had never really questioned the notion that God was with me, inside of me, and looking out for me. I had liked having that knowledge tucked in my pocket. But now it was gone, just like that. And there in the sand, kneeling, there was no Jacob in me, wrestling with the angel or demanding my miracle. I didn't play God a boom-box serenade of Peter Gabriel's "In Your Eyes," begging for him to take me back.

I wonder sometimes if losing one's faith is an unavoidable outcome of taking a belief, any belief, to its logical conclusion, of following the example of Icarus and flying too close to the sun, if you will. Years later, I viewed alchemy as the metaphor with which to understand what happened to my faith. Even after they came to know the truth, alchemists continued to toil away on their impossible quest to turn base metal into gold. Likewise, perhaps salvation was to be found in the journey. Not for me though. I hightailed it out of there as soon as I felt God leave me, and I barely looked back.

In retrospect, I fear I was relieved.

Years later, my wife's college friend, Lucas, came to visit us in Prague. He was going through a major spiritual crisis. Like me, he had been an evangelical, a teenage preacher. And he had come to the conclusion that he didn't believe in Jesus or even God anymore. We hit it off, as you can imagine. One night, drunk, he told me his greatest fear about losing his religion. It was not that he would be alone in the universe or that he would no longer have a purpose in life. It was that he might discover he had never believed in the first place. I had never considered such a proposition before. I have never forgotten it since.

The Movement

*   *   *   *   *
  *   *   *   *
*   *   *   *   *

A Brand-New Jungle

I'll see you on the dark side of the moon.

Pink Floyd, "Brain Damage"

Before Costa Rica, I had a plan for my life. I would graduate from Goshen and enter a Mennonite seminary to become a minister. I would marry Erma and together we would run a church in some small town in Iowa, Indiana, or Ohio. She would be the kind-hearted youth pastor and choir director, and I would be the earnest preacher, inspiring others and doing God's good work.

Unfortunately, Erma was no longer my patient and understanding girlfriend. She, quite understandably, had had enough. When I returned from Costa Rica, she and I went for a walk in the college gardens. She informed me, if I hadn't guessed already, that it was over.

Moreover, now that the whole "God thing" suddenly seemed preposterous to me, all my plans were changing. I viewed my final trimesters at Goshen as a trial. The prospect of attending mandatory chapel sessions three times a week, taking religious classes, and hanging out with believers felt all wrong.

With my parents holed up in Alaska, I had no family to visit over the holidays, so I stayed on campus with a smattering of exchange students, resigned to serving my time until graduation. But then two guys on my dorm floor asked if I wanted to drive with them to New York City to see the ball drop on New Year's Eve. Hell yeah, why not?

My traveling companions knew a woman there, Stephanie, who worked as a nanny for Steven Stills (of Crosby, Stills, Nash, and Young fame). She was a Mennonite, too, a Goshen native who'd graduated a few years earlier from Eastern Mennonite College and moved to New York. She'd let us crash at her place. Perfect.

When we walked into her small Manhattan apartment, she set down her cigarette and ran to hug her friends. She had a nose ring and smelled of patchouli. When we were introduced she hugged me, too, and just like that I was smitten. She was a broad-shouldered hippie who smoked weed and listened to the Dead, and our first evening at her apartment was grand. Everyone drank or got high but me, for while God was gone, my old morality lingered, though I *almost* had some champagne. The next morning, the others went out to get bagels and coffee while Stephanie and I snuggled in bed. Pretty soon I was breathing in the smell of her hair, and she began to touch me. We had sex—one sin at a time, I guess—which was my first sexual contact since the almost-sex disaster at the Hospitality Community and my first real intercourse since the incident in Shannon's dorm years earlier. It blew me away, and afterward, she didn't scream or punch pillows or throw me out of a window. I watched her, mystified, as she rolled a joint naked. We talked. She told me about how she was bored with the church and fed up with its patriarchy. I told her about my dissipating belief and the feeling that God had abandoned me. It felt like an adult conversation, one I'd probably not have again until graduation.

About a month after my New York trip, Stephanie moved back to Goshen to work for her brother, who ran a tanning salon in town. The day she arrived, she asked me out. I happily accepted, and Stephanie and I began a mutually beneficial relationship of screwing, talking, and, eventually, sharing her apartment, as my twenty-first birthday that January meant I was no longer subject to Goshen's policies regarding off-campus living. Stephanie liked acid and marijuana, and though I didn't partake, I saw that drugs weren't inherently evil. When high, Stephanie would listen to me and help me take stock of my life. And here was my situation: in the spring, I'd be a twenty-one-year-old atheist with a deeply religious background, a loud-talking bag of nerves under doctor's orders to take lithium and thorazine. I was a little angry in a way young men can be, but mostly I was thirsty for adventure. I wanted to see the world. But what was I going to do? And what in the world did I believe was worth doing?

In May, my academic advisor told me about a program I might like. The Brethren Church ran something called the Brethren Voluntary Service, which set up young college grads with mission work around the world. This sounded like the last thing I wanted, but she insisted that being a Christian wasn't a prerequisite to entering the organization. The BVS was more like the Peace Corps, she explained, and as I thumbed through brochures of current job listings, one for an environmental youth organization in the Netherlands caught my eye. A job in Europe, with my lodging, food, health insurance, and a stipend for minor expenses covered by a church group? That sounded fantastic! One night at Stephanie's, with her encouraging me all the way, I filled out the application. Within weeks I was accepted. I now had a job waiting for me after graduation.

⁓

When I arrived at the European Youth Forest Action's headquarters in Sittard, a city of about forty thousand souls in the south of Holland, I was in many ways free. Stephanie and I ended things with no fuss; I cried a bit but she tousled my hair and told me to go have an adventure. My family was tucked away in Alaska. I had no home base, no money, and no religion. My possessions, half of which were mixed tapes, fit neatly into an army duffel bag. I arrived at the airport ready to take on the world, dressed in a sarong, with a ponytail running down the middle of my back and a peace sign dangling from my ear.

Crossing the Atlantic felt like a transformative experience for me. The water below was like the water in the baptismal many years ago or the water I'd stared at during that transformative party in Costa Rica. Crossing over that water could change me.

Or rather, it reminded me that I could change myself. I could define and create my own life. I could be anything I wanted to be. And to prove it, I got up, walked to the plane's bathroom, and dumped my canister of thorazine into the trash can.

I had never liked thorazine. Which is not surprising. Who in their right mind daily ingests a medication nicknamed "the chemical lobotomy"? I felt I couldn't change if I kept taking it. Lithium was different: it evened out my highs and lows, and it kept me from staring into cupboards and wanting to crawl in. But I felt—and feared—that thorazine dampened my risk threshold. I was twenty-one and on my way to Europe. I wanted a little risk, not limited horizons. I knew that I had been in crisis and had nearly broken down at Goshen. I desperately needed psychiatry. But I had my limits. Was the solution a lifetime of soma? A brave new world of numbness? Did I really have to suppress large parts of myself to amplify the parts that society accepted? For a fledging atheist and aspiring hippie who was about to start working for a radical environmental organization in Europe, that didn't sound cool at all.

There was also my vanity to consider. A side effect from certain psychiatric medications, including thorazine, was that I'd rock back and forth, ever so slightly, while sitting. Imagine trying to impress a young lady while simultaneously knowing that your behavior mirrors that of asylum patients you'd seen in *One Flew Over the Cuckoo's Nest*. If this was a short-term fix—a cast on a broken leg that would eventually be removed—I could have lived with it. But there was no end in sight to my problems.

I realize now that I was indeed overmedicated, that psychiatry was at the time—and still is—overzealous about doling out pills. I have struggled with my meds my whole life—which ones to take and how much.

At the time, I didn't realize I would never take thorazine again. That moment on the plane marked my own small rebellion. An offering to the gods of the new me.

—⁓⁓—

EYFA's headquarters were located in a two-story building over-looking a pedestrians-only plaza on the outskirts of Sittard. We worked on the first floor and lived on the second. Our neighbors included an alternative printing press, a small theater that also ran a bar and coffee shop, an organic vegan cooperative, and an anarchist housing and cooking collective called Rampemplan. At lunch time or during other breaks, the outdoor tables of the plaza filled with these organizations' misfit employees.

Inside EYFA there was a righteous zeal, as our collective mission was to save the environment and, by extension, the planet. The folks I met told stories about being buried up to their necks in the ground as they tried to stop bulldozers from flattening the Sarawak jungle in Indonesia. Some had been imprisoned fighting to end the Soviet Union. Others had worked on Greenpeace's *Rainbow Warrior*. They were vegan. They were tattooed and pierced. They were dirty and hard. They were amazing.

The staff comprised ten hippies from all over Europe, who lived and worked full time in an anarchist collective. Our office was ground zero for the entire organization that spanned the conti-nent. It was 1991, and I wasn't the only new kid in town. Recruits were pouring in from former Communist countries. Wide-eyed kids from East Berlin or Kiev or Sofia would arrive with sleeping bags and a shitload of desires. On any given night, there were two dozen of them crashing at EYFA, and they all wanted to test-drive their newfound freedom from the Soviet Union. Sure, they wanted the training we offered in environmental education, nonviolent resistance, grant writing, and technology instruction, tools that would ostensibly help them improve their EYFA-affiliate back home. But they also wanted to do drugs and try on Levi's jeans and fuck and listen to rock and roll turned up to eleven. On that score, I could relate.

My job was to serve as editor-in-chief of the organization's monthly magazine, which required me to assign and edit articles from EYFA activists across Europe. Eventually, I also supervised the design and layout for the magazine, and I tackled longer, more in-depth feature articles and editorials, too. The job required a lot of travel and meetings with young activists around Europe. In many ways, the work reminded me of the Hospitality Community and the sanctuary movement, but without the religion. To say I was psyched would be an understatement. I was overworked and underpaid. I was in over my head. I traveled almost constantly. Everything was new. I was surrounded by passionate people and true believers. In other words, I was in heaven.

At my first communal meal at EYFA, I had my first beer, my first vegan meal, and my first drugs. The cauliflower stir-fry with brown rice tasted exotic, and it took me forever to drink the beer, which I found very strong. After the meal, I struck up a conversation with Paxus Calta, the only other American working at EYFA. He was about ten years older than me and very tall, lanky, and dirty. After dinner he handed me a hash pipe. I took it without hesitation and, without asking what it was, smoked it. As I floated away in a haze Paxus whispered in my ear, "Welcome home." It was as if he knew where I'd come from and where I'd be going.

———

Paxus and I immediately hit it off, and the next day he insisted I attend a meeting with him in Eindhoven, about forty miles north of Sittard. We could stay with his wife, he said, a "friend" he'd married so he could obtain a Dutch green card. I don't recall the meeting at all but remember going back to her flat and feeling like a third wheel. Those two were certainly more than friends. To give them some space, I told them I wanted to walk around and check out the city. I grabbed some money and my passport, and just before I left, Paxus handed me a hand-rolled spliff—a mix of crumbled hash and tobacco—and a Walkman with a Pink Floyd cassette in it. "You're going to need these," he said.

I smoked half the joint in the breezeway and, without further ado, headed straight for the city's red-light district.

Before arriving in Holland, I didn't know about its loose laws governing prostitution or drugs. But now that I did, I wanted to try it. All of it.

High as hell, I walked and pondered the simple, brutal beauty before me: women in negligees standing behind glass doors with red lights in them, each willing to accept fifty guilders to have sex with me. I had enjoyed sex with Stephanie, but as I walked around listening to the *Dark Side of the Moon* (an album, I must add, I had never even heard of) I wanted to fuck. I wanted desperately to sin. Really sin. I wanted a clean break from God. I didn't want to be violent or steal or hurt others, but I wanted to do something wrong. I wanted to be bad. This had nothing to do with my medication; the thorazine still hadn't completely left my system. It was much more simple. This was between me and God.

I shopped like a chauvinist-pig pervert. And I didn't care. I picked a woman with the biggest breasts I could find. I asked her how much it would cost to have another woman who looked like her join us. She laughed and returned with a friend. I paid them with glee from the stipend I was given by the Brethren Church— reveling in the poetic justice of it all. Once I was alone in a room with them, stoned and ridiculously horny, I went crazy. I asked them to do everything I had ever thought of—things to me, things to each other. It was fantastic.

A new me, devoid of Christianity's spoon-fed morality, emerged from those red lights. And as I walked away I decided to get some schwarma and fries and see what other debaucheries this small town had to offer. I reached in my jacket for Paxus's Walkman. It was gone. So was my passport and all my money. I laughed. "More poetic justice" I thought. In the bottom of my front pocket I found the other half of the joint. I was plenty high already, but I bummed a light from a homeless guy and smoked it with him anyway. Too stoned to even see clearly or walk straight I found a nearby park bench, lay down, and stared at the drizzle as it hit my glasses until dawn. I might have been humming "Welcome to the Jungle" the whole time for all I know.

In the Bush Leagues

This interview aired on the public radio show *This American Life*, produced by WBEZ Chicago, Episode 257: "What I Should've Said." © 2004 Ira Glass and Chicago Public Media.

—*mm*—

Ira Glass: When he was in his early twenties, barely out of school, at the very first political event of his life, Charles Monroe-Kane got into a shouting match with the leader of the free world. And he pretty much lost that one. This was in the early 1990s. He just left the religious school where he had been studying to be a minister. And he moved to Amsterdam, where he fell in with a bunch of anarchists. He edited an environmental newspaper called the *Green Tree News*.

Charles Monroe-Kane: And I wanted to be an activist, so that's the whole reason I think I wanted to be a minister. I was into liberation theology. That's what I wanted to be.

And I was there about four or five weeks. And the G7 meeting was happening in Munich, Germany. President Bush—former President Bush, or President Senior, or Dad, whatever you want to call him—he was president. So we went down like a good activist would do. It was in Munich, Germany. We went down to protest. And I had only been doing this for four or five weeks, so I was kind of down.

It was my first political action ever. I was sleeping in the back of a bus with a bunch of dreadlocked people. I had my hair down over my shoulders, and I had just gotten my ear pierced. I had a peace sign in my earring. You can imagine the person, right?

And so basically, we were going down to protest, and I had this press pass. I'm a bit of a talker, bit of a schmoozer. Met some people there, and found out that there are seven levels of press passes. I had level number one, which got you nothing but some faxes. Level number two got you nothing but some faxes, but also got you this buffet once a day. And now I'm sleeping in a bus. I'm like, well, hell, I'm not stupid. So I fandango my way in—press pass number two.

Well, of course, food brought me to number three and number four. Now, number five got you a hotel room. I thought, well, my friends could use this. Because we were starting to smell on the second day. So I kept BS-ing my way all the way through just to get these press passes.

Ira: Wait, so you get the room?

Charles: All the way to the sixth level, yeah. I get the room. We get in there—and the food was awesome, by the way, on the sixth level—and the suite was—it was a decent—it was almost like a suite. It was a decent size where all of us could stay for free.

And then what happens is I'm with some people who later became very good friends of mine, but at the time, I didn't know them very well. A friend named Paxus and some others who were high level at Friends of the Earth and Greenpeace. These people are like, "Do you realize what you have? You have a level-six press pass at the G7 meeting. You have access to all these places and all these things."

"OK, that's cool."

He said, "But what you don't have is you don't have a White House press pass. That's the top level." So he's like, "You know what you ought to do? You ought to try the next level. You should try to get a White House press pass."

I said, "Why?"

He said, "Because you could be live at a press conference. You can protest. Tomorrow, George Bush, at 11 o'clock in the morning"—this is in the afternoon the day before—"he's giving a live press conference on CNN."

I was like, "Oh, I never thought of it. I've never done an action before."

So I went, and I went to this beer garden where I knew some of the people who made the decisions were. And I met a man named Marlin Fitzwater—I think a lot of people might know who he is—and he's sitting there drinking. But I didn't know who the hell he was.

Ira: The White House press secretary.

Charles: Yeah, yeah.

Ira: The actual White House press secretary.

Charles: Because that's the step. Because that's a higher level. The president's got a different security issue.

Well, here's the logic for him, right? He's already assumed I've been checked. Remember, he already knows I have the sixth-level press pass, so I'm not like I'm an anarchist in Amsterdam or something like that, for Christ's sake. So I think that he wasn't too worried about that.

So then, anyway, he gives me a press pass. It's very exciting. I go back to my hotel room with a bunch of naked, dirty hippies, and I show these people the press pass. And they flip out. They're like, "You're kidding. You got it." I don't understand the ramifications of what's about to happen at all. So basically, they're like, "Well, tomorrow morning, President Bush, at 11 o'clock in the morning, is giving this conference, a press conference live on CNN. You should—you have a press pass to go there—I think that you should do something."

I was like, "Well, I agree."

So then I sit down with these guys, these guys now who are like—all the hippie, dirty activists are out of the room, and now I've got the Greenpeace, Friends of the Earth people who know what they're talking about guys. And they're like, "Have you thought about what you're going to say?"

And I was like, "No, not really."

So we talked about it. And they said, "The most important thing to do is two things. Keep your hands away from your body while you do this, so you don't get shot. Because they might think it's an attempted assassination or something.

And you're going to get twenty to thirty seconds max. That's all you're going to get, so know what you're going to say."

Ira: Wait, wait. These are the two pieces of advice they give you? Piece of advice number one is, don't get yourself shot? Like, that's—

Charles: It's good advice, though. And I took it. Because they were like, "Keep your hands away from your body." They said, "Don't wear a watch. Roll up your sleeves, or have on a short-sleeve shirt. You have to be careful. You're in a small room. You're standing up—basically, you're going to stand up on a chair. Situate yourself in the middle of the room, so you're hard to get at by the Secret Service guys, who are going to, in fifteen or thirty seconds, drag you away and arrest you. So what are you going to say?"

And I thought, "Well, all I know is Christianity."

And they said, "Well, that's OK. You can go with that. Americans relate to that."

And I said, "You know, I've always wanted to be one of the Old Testament prophets. I thought that would be really cool. That's kind of a life dream. That was what I wanted to be."

Ira: Now, wait, wait. Now when you say this to a bunch of real activists, "I've always wanted to be one of the Old Testament prophets," is that pretty much where they roll their eyes and slowly shake their heads and look at the ground? They just think, "Oh, what have we gotten ourselves into here?"

Charles: No, I think they were more like, "Jesus, this dude's got a White House press pass in his hand, and he is such an idiot. He's so not prepared that we've got to help this kid out. Because we don't have the press pass. He does, and he's the only one who's going to get in."

And so I went to the Bible. And my favorite prophet was Jeremiah. And Jeremiah had a certain style. So I think, "Here's what I want to do. I want to get some ashes. I'm going to put some ashes on my head. I want to rip my shirt off, rip it open [*makes ripping sound*] like that. And I'm going to give him a line from the Old Testament. A good line."

And they said, "Well, maybe you shouldn't quote the Bible. You should do it in that style, something from your thing."

So I thought about it, thought about it, and I came up with this great line. "The homeless in the trees are mourning your economic decisions. Repent, dear King, or go to hell." I thought, "Now, that's a good line." That's good. It's about him, but it takes inanimate objects into effect. I'm an environmental activist as well. So I said, "That's what I'm going to do."

Ira: Now Charles, can we just pause the story right here—

Charles: Absolutely.

Ira: And let's move to the present, a dozen years later. Now, when you think about that quote now, as the adult you are, how do you view that quote now?

Charles: Oh my god, it's the most embarrassing choice of anything I would ever use in my life. If I had thirty seconds to choose now, I think I would say something maybe a little bit more, a little less, whatever—symbolic, I don't know. But that's what I had. I was twenty-two, and that's all I knew.

So I practiced it over and over again. "The homeless in the trees are mourning your economic decisions. Repent, dear King, or go to hell. The homeless in the trees are mourning your economic decisions. Repent, dear King, or go to hell." Hands away from my body.

But then one of the activist guys came up with a great idea, this American guy. He was like, "Well, don't rip your clothes because that's going to get misunderstood. You should rip an American flag in half. And that should be the cloth that you rip."

I said, "That's a great idea." So I'm going to put ashes on my forehead, I'm going to rip an American flag in half, I'm going to read that statement, yell it out with all the passion I can muster, get arrested, and awesome!

Ira: Wait. Have you ever—you've lived in the United States of America, right?

Charles: Yeah.

Ira: Are you familiar with how people feel about the ripping in half of the American flag?

Charles: That's probably part of the reason he liked and I liked it, I think, at the time.

Ira: But weren't you trying to win the sympathies of your countrymen?

Charles: Yeah, I think I was. But I also think I was—I don't know what I was trying to do, man—I was twenty-two. When you were twenty-two, did you know what you were trying to do? Good Lord, I don't know what I was trying to do.

So I couldn't sleep that night. They were right. I couldn't sleep. I was a little nervous. And they got me a shirt and a pair of pants. Some shoes that fit me. We had to go to different activists to find it all. A nice tie. I took the earring out. They had a lawyer for me. I gave him my passport. Nothing in my pockets. But shoved down the front of my pants is an American flag—partly ripped on the top, so I could easily rip it in half— and some ashes in my pocket.

And this quote burned into my brain. It was like a zen— I don't even know what zen is at the time—I do now. But at the time, it was a zen mantra. "The homeless in the trees are mourning your economic decisions. Repent, dear King, or go to hell." And that's all I had in my mind.

So I go into the press conference saying, you know—and a former Christian kid, here I am. So I sit down. I situate myself in the middle of the room. There's about forty-four, forty-five people. And I remember counting them. I was nervous, so I counted all the people. My throat was dry, and I thought I was going to pass out. And I didn't want to throw up. I knew that would be bad. That wouldn't be a good symbol. And I didn't want to pass out.

So it's coming up to the point. My heart's aflutter.

Ira: Well, let me stop you right there. Because we have here in the studio a videotape of this day, July 8, 1992. We got this courtesy of the Vanderbilt University Television Archives. And you have never seen this?

Charles: No, I've never seen it. I've never even seen the highlights from any of the news. All I've seen is newspaper stuff. I'm really nervous about watching this.

Ira: OK. Let's roll the tape.

News anchor: Right now, let's go live to Munich to hear President Bush's comments at the close of the G7 summit.

Charles: I totally remember that, him coming in. That was intense.

President George H. W. Bush:—the last three days discussing the responsibilities and opportunities that we had—

Charles: Because that's the point where I'm sitting there with a flag between my legs I'm going rip in half and yell at the man, the President of the United States. Oh my god, it makes me want to pass out. All right. Sorry.

President Bush:—sustaining political reform. I would cite five key accomplishments at the Munich Economic Summit. We've succeeded in achieving a solid consensus on strengthening—

Ira: Now, he's barely spoken for a half minute. He's still in his opening statement.

President Bush:—United States, Japan, [*yelling in the background*] Germany, and Italy have—

Ira: Now the camera's panning back.

Charles: Repent. We mourn your decisions here. You're not giving us your voice.

Charles: Oh my god, look at that kid. Wow, you can't even hear the great line, "The homeless in the trees are mourning your decisions here."

Ira: You can't hear it all. You can't hear it at all. All you hear is the president.

Charles: Oh, I didn't even notice that. I didn't even know that. What if nobody heard it? I guess not. This is the tape.

Ira: This is the tape. I don't think anybody heard it.

Charles: Wow. That's intense.

President Bush: I'm trying to give—

Charles: [*inaudible*] your voice in the U.S.

President Bush: I'm trying to give you my voice right now. And if you'd be quiet, maybe you could hear it.

Charles: But you're not giving it to us [*inaudible*].

President Bush: Well, would you please sit down? We're in the middle of a press conference here.

Charles: You're not giving us your voice there.

President Bush: Well, what's your question, sir?

Charles: I'm under twenty-five, and I want to know—

President Bush: Well, we can tell that.

Charles: Nice. Good for him. He got me on that one.

President Bush: Now, what's your question?

Charles: Now, this I remember. Because I just assumed I was going to be arrested. I knew I wasn't going to be shot. That hadn't happened yet, so that's cool. And I'm like, "This is it." And what happened next was amazing because nothing happened next.

I didn't get arrested. He had this thing where he had his hands on the podium, and he kind of moved his hands. I don't know what signals they have, or whatever, but they didn't arrest me. And then the worst possible thing in the world happened to me. He ain't going to arrest me, and he's about to engage me. And I was like, "Oh my god. The President of the United States is speaking to me right now." And he basically started asking me questions. And I was like, "Holy mackerel." I really almost passed out.

President Bush: Who are you, and who are you accredited to?

Charles: My name is Charles Kane.

President Bush: Yeah.

Charles: I'm from the United States.

President Bush: Yeah.

Charles: I work with a magazine in the Netherlands. It's a youth magazine. And we want to know why we're not taken seriously. We're an environmental group.

President Bush: Well, maybe you're rude. People don't take rude people seriously. And if you interrupt a press conference like this, I'm sure that people would say that's why we don't take you seriously.

Charles: [*inaudible*].

President Bush: Sit down, and I will take a question from you when we get in the question and answer period. Right now, I would like to continue my statement with your permission.

Charles: Thank you, Captain. Go ahead.

President Bush: Now, where were we? We were talking about economic recovery [*chuckles*].

Ira: So the president gives this little nervous laugh and sort of looks down, and then he goes on with his regular statement.

Charles: Oh my god.

Ira: And this continues for a few minutes.

Charles: So I'm sitting down, that's all. I don't remember.

Ira: So you're sitting down.

Charles: Why didn't I keep yelling? What a wimp. I guess I was probably—but he gave me a cue there.

Ira: Well, what do you mean why—What he was saying was perfectly reasonable. "I'll get to you during the question—look, we're going to talk, and it's going to be during the question and answer period. I'm just reading my opening statement." How are you going to argue with that?

Charles: Yeah, but it's a protest. I was supposed to be in there yelling at him. I was supposed to get arrested. I thought I was supposed to get arrested.

Oh my god, I so didn't want to be there after I didn't get arrested. I was so embarrassed. It was horrible.

Ira: Because from your point of view, the whole point was to get arrested.

Charles: Yes.

Ira: So now at this point, you've failed.

Charles: Well, also, I not only failed at that point for not getting arrested, I also know I'm going to fail because he's going to ask a question to me later. Because I don't have anything to say. I mean, you've got to remember that. I don't have anything to say. I don't have a question. What do you mean, I have a question? Of course, I don't have a question.

Ira: So finally it comes to you. You're the third question. And basically, he answers two questions, and then he says this.

President Bush: And that's what we're talking about. Now, let's go to this gentleman who's so agitated here.

Charles: I just want to know why there's no new nuclear power plants in the United States being built, but you're proposing for Siemens to build them in Eastern Europe?

President Bush: Oh, I'd like some more to be built.

Charles: Why are they so unsafe in our country and so safe in their country?

President Bush: Well, I don't think they're un—

Charles: Why it is only at the G7—

President Bush: You've asked your question, sir. Now let me try to answer it for you. I favor nuclear power. I believe that it can be safely used. I believe that it is environmentally sound. The debate here has been that we ought to try to help those areas that have nuclear facilities that might not have the latest technology and might not meet the same standards of safety that we use in our country. Thank you very much. Now, we'll go here.

Charles: Do you respect the flag?

Ira: Then you said, "Do you respect the flag?"

President Bush: You had your question.

Charles: Oh, now the media is yelling at me.

[*crowd yelling.*]

Charles: It's all rhetoric. Come on, you guys, think about it.

Ira: And then you say, "It's all rhetoric."

Charles: Is the world going to be a better place in a year?

President Bush: This is coming out of your time, gang, and we've got twenty minutes here.

Media member: This is a press conference, man.

Charles: Come on. This [*unintelligible*] acting up at all.

Sam Donaldson: Mr. President—

Charles: You guys are all part of this system too.

Ira: And then the president sort of laughs.

Charles: Thanks a lot. Go ahead.

Sam Donaldson: Much has been said here by you and others about the—

Charles: We've given up.

Ira: And then there's the voice of Sam Donaldson. And then now, it's back to normal.

Charles: God, I can't believe I did that. That's embarrassing. It's so hot in here. I'm totally embarrassed by that. Oh my god. I mean, I'm not embarrassed about yelling at the President of the United States. I do not sit here right now and say, "Wow, I wish I wouldn't have done it." No way. I sit here right now and say, "I wish I would have done it better."

Ira: And what would doing a better job have meant? What do you wish that you would have said?

Charles: I wish I would have said something that kind of hung in the air for a moment, that made everybody silent, that would keep him awake for one moment of his life, that just would make him think, "Wow, I do have some responsibility, and I have squandered that responsibility."

Ira: But what could that possibly be?

Charles: I don't know. Haven't you been touched by one statement in your life that's affected you greatly? I have.

Ira: Yes, but it's—

Charles: So I'm giving him credit.

Ira: It seems very unlikely in this setting.

Charles: Now, in retrospect, it's extremely unlikely. It's probably a million to one, but you got to try. You got to try.

Ira: I don't know. When I see the president answering questions at a news conference, I feel like what he's doing is—he doesn't want to say anything that's going to get him in trouble. He doesn't want to say anything that's going to make his life more complicated and difficult. And it's not an environment conducive to learning.

Charles: What I should have said is—when I think about it at 3 o'clock in the morning, it's not the—it's in general what I should have said. I should have said something that would affect the man's life. And what's depressing for me that really makes me sad is that I still haven't come up with what I should have said. And that really makes me sad.

Ira: But of course, you didn't come up with what you should have said because nothing could have been said—

Charles: I won't accept that—

Ira: In that setting that was going to make the President of the United States rethink anything in particular.

Charles: I won't accept that. I should have found something that could have changed the world at that moment. I had my opportunity at that moment. I think I should have gone for it.

Ira: Now, you're in your thirties now. Have you ever had this experience where somebody just yelled something at you, some punk kid, whatever, yelled at you?

Charles: I did. I was at an introduction. I was introducing somebody who was about to give a speech. They heckled me. It was a really interesting experience because immediately what came back was me.

Ira: Did it keep you up at night afterwards? Did it give you something to think about?

Charles: That's an unfair—of course, no, it didn't give me anything to think about. No, it didn't keep me up at night at all. It didn't—yeah, I get your—that's a good question. No, it didn't keep me up at all.

Ira: And so do you think, thinking about George Bush and the possibility that he would be kept up at night by a moment like this—

Charles: No. No, OK, I understand where you're going. I respect where you're going. No, of course not. But I know this all along. Yeah, I know this all along. It's only what you wish would have happened. I hope—I don't know. Maybe I'll read his memoirs, and he'll say, "You know—"

OK, forget it. I won't even go there. I tried, man. It was a tough day, man. It was a tough day. I tried really. I did my best. My best wasn't very good at the time, but I tried my best.

Bye-Bye Leather Pants

I'm sittin' down here in the campfire light,
Waitin' on the ghost of Tom Joad.

Bruce Springsteen, "The Ghost of Tom Joad"

Hey, aren't you the guy who threw a pencil at President Bush?" she asked, with stars in her eyes and a flower in her hair.

Because there was no internet yet to circulate the actual video of my presidential encounter, my Bush story endured a few rounds of telephone around the environmental movement. And I might have sprinkled in an exaggeration or two to tamp down the reality that I was made to appear a dunce in front of the free world. The new version ended with me heroically throwing a pencil at the president and shouting in exasperation, "Do you love whales?" which made me a political activist rock star to many, including to this young lady, who immediately gave me a blow job. A blow job! For yelling at the president of the United States! Far out!

———

By now I was splitting time between Sittard and Amsterdam. Paxus had a flat in the big city that doubled as an EYFA satellite office, so when I got sick of consensus decision making in Sittard or the tribulations of living in the anarchist chaos, I would take a train to Amsterdam and work and live there for a week or two.

The flat was small but nice, basically four tidy rooms with a closet near the front door, which is where I'd sleep. The floor plan was odd. A door in the main room led to Paxus's bedroom, but to access the kitchen and the bathroom, you had to pass through Paxus's room. Now, Paxus was not a discreet man and had few, if any, inhibitions, so it was not uncommon to stroll through his room while he was copulating with one of his many girlfriends. I didn't particularly love doing that, and one day, while sitting on the toilet looking at the wall in front of me, I had a realization. This wall was not connected to Paxus's bedroom; it was connected to the main room.

No one was home, so I grabbed a crow bar and got to work. After a few bong hits, a bottle of Jägermeister, and lots of Rage Against the Machine, I'd created a huge hole and an even bigger mess. Paxus's face was priceless the next day when he saw not only the three-by-four-foot hole in his bathroom wall but a solid inch of dust on just about every one of his possessions. Eventually, I cleaned up the place, but the jagged opening grew in legend after a young activist came up from Sittard and painted the world's most god-awful mural around it. Central to her creation were two gaudy, life-size images of Ace, a rather large black man from Curacao who worked for EYFA, and another colleague, Yan, an equally large white woman from Denmark. They were portrayed as Greek gods. Henceforth, Paxus's flat became known as "the hole in the wall."

—⁓—

Perhaps it's the narcissist in me talking, but Amsterdam felt like it was a place built just for me at that time in my life. And it wasn't just because of the weed that I was now smoking daily or the experiments with Ecstasy and LSD; I also believed in the cause of EYFA and the environmental movement. The more I learned about clear-cut forests and nuclear power and poisoned drinking water and needless highway projects and emerging ideas surrounding climate change, the more I became enraged and wanted action. I worked very hard. I still edited EYFA's newspaper, the *Green Tree News*, and I soon was named co-organizer of EYFA's largest yearly event: Ecotopia.

Every summer, thousands of college-aged activists from across Europe would gather for six weeks to share notes and plan the revolution. The entire event was vegan and idealistic and pure—the spirit among the participants was very similar to and as unrealistic as the spirit I'd encountered among the missionaries in the Philippines and Haiti. I believed, you see, that you could change the world through a summer ecotopia with a bunch of hippies. Why not? The world as it was certainly wasn't working.

Ecotopia was based on the seminal 1974 utopian novel by Ernest Callenbach, an unrealistic manifesto that is set in a future where a group of humans live in a creative world without war or environmental degradation. The book values creativity, espouses equality for women, and calls for taking the steps necessary to ensure the restoration of the ecosystem. It promotes peer-to-peer learning, direct democracy, friendliness, and, not least, play. In other words, it was completely awesome. Just going to such an event, let alone helping to plan it, was like a dream for me. This year's gathering was to be in Bulgaria. I was going to help make it the best Ecotopia ever.

By this point, my newfound loss of Christian morality had opened me up to trying just about anything, including polyamory, which only months earlier would have blown my mind. It was Paxus who explained the logic of it. Love is exponential: Why bottle it up by limiting yourself to one person?

Good point, Paxus!

Enter Abelone and Ingrid.

Abelone, a gorgeous brunette from Denmark, lived in Sittard and was a married mother of two children. Her husband had founded EYFA but was now off in Serbia, trying to stop the war there. His activism bordered on the maniacal. By the time I showed up he was out of the picture. Still, Abelone was attracted to true believers and there I was—a shining light of idealist Truth. Though she barely spoke English, our relationship was all consuming from the moment we met on my first day at EYFA.

Ingrid, meanwhile, was a cute and chubby blonde Norwegian grad student and EYFA activist. Her work brought her down to the EYFA offices often, where she had a room next to mine. Her breasts floored me, but her intellect sealed the deal. She was one of the original thinkers and researchers on climate change, an idea that had not yet come to be widely known. In her quiet and subtle way, she filled my head, and my heart, with radical ideas.

It was freeing to be honest with each woman about the other and to be able to make love to one one day and the other the next without guilt. So much of sex was guilt, I realized. Sex rocked. Guilt sucked. Such simple realizations! And they led me to many more sexual encounters outside of Ingrid and Abelone as well. It felt like something inside of me was expanding with each one.

And then there were drugs. I fully embraced the notion that my doors of perception needed opening. Weed kept my mania under control and had the totally awesome side effect of getting me stoned. I cut my lithium dose in half and smoked pot twice a day instead. The fact that I had also recently quit my thorazine entirely and was now experimenting with recreational drugs was affecting my mind. I had psychotic episodes. I started hearing voices again—though only on occasions. But I was surrounded by people who actually *celebrated my weirdness*. In doing so, I felt they were celebrating me. I did, soon after, go back to my original dose of lithium. But I felt empowered, and I believed I knew myself enough to medicate on my own terms.

And medicate myself I did.

Ecstasy was reserved for extreme pleasure seeking. It also helped me discover the joys of letting repetitive, loud techno music penetrate your brain. I found that nothing goes better together than music, random sex, and Ecstasy. Nothing!

But what fascinated me most at the time was LSD. I felt that an LSD trip was similar, in some ways, to an ecstatic Christian experience. Acid simultaneously seemed to reveal and free me from all the bullshit and lies I'd endured as an evangelical. The socially constructed walls imposed on me by the church, my education, and my culture were being torn down (thank you, Jericho!). And new doors were opening—doors I could choose to open or close. I was probably insufferable to those around me—all these daily revelations pouring out of me—but dammit, my mind *was* being blown. And I was becoming something new.

With my new life came new routines. One of my favorites was hanging out with Paxus at the Wall in Amsterdam. It was a coffee shop near our flat that played Pink Floyd's film *The Wall* on repeat. They made killer strawberry smoothies, and we would sip them, fucked up on space cake, while we watched Pink cut his nipple and shave the hair off of his chest. We must have seen that movie a thousand times. One day, after dropping several hits of acid, we were in the Wall to get a joint and catch a few scenes when it dawned on us that there were very loud noises coming from the street. We got up to investigate. Marching past the door was a high school band. And then another. And another. It was a fucking marching-band parade going right through the red light district.

For you stoners and trippers out there, I need not explain further. You understand how fantastically wonderful this would be. If you have never been so high that you couldn't remember where (or what) your lighter was, let me explain. It is like suddenly being granted a life-long wish without asking for it or even realizing how desperately you wanted such a thing, then marveling at the fact that the karma gods would grant you it. It's mind-numbingly confusing and absolutely perfect.

Obviously, we followed the parade.

We ended up in Vondelpark in the center of Amsterdam. It was raining, as usual, and, at some point, we realized the music had gone away. Yes, we were so high that we lost a parade of marching bands. We wandered to a special spot Paxus knew about, a section of the park where you could no longer hear the sounds of the city. We laid down in the rain and enjoyed the pitter patter on our bodies. Soon a parrot landed near Paxus. A full-on, full-color parrot straight out of the Amazon rain forest. This was wonderful, even after we remembered we did not live in a rain forest. We studied the bird for several minutes before realizing it had company. We were tripping so hard that reality was slipping away, but dammit, these were real parrots! And soon there were a dozen at least! Then I saw her: a bag lady with a shopping cart full of birdseed. The parrots—who knows where they came from—were gathering around her as she fed them. She saw us, understood, and smiled. We couldn't fathom communicating with her, so we just laid back down. I closed my eyes. After what seemed liked hours but was certainly only minutes, I could feel the rain again, though now it was more irregular and, well, not wet. I opened my eyes and peered down at my chest. I was covered in birdseed. Timidly at first, the birds began to land and eat the seeds off of me. Within minutes I was being devoured. I know that drug stories can be tedious, but please allow me this indulgence to say that every peck was like a dot being connected in my mind. Every constellation of dots opened a new door.

This was it. This was the unexpected pure romantic beauty that I craved. Something that proved that the nature of things was innately good. That there was an original blessing quite different from the original sin I'd been taught about. That even though there was no God, there was a purpose. And these moments of exhilarating madness reinforced somehow that I was on the correct path, that no longer believing in God was the right decision and that drugs could take an atheist above and beyond the normal physical experience of life. That transcendence was possible — even for the fallen.

～～～

After months of organizing and fund-raising, Ecotopia Bulgaria was only a few weeks away. More than a thousand youth had registered, and a bike tour of some 350 college students was already pedaling its way from London. The anarchist organization from my Sittard plaza, Rampenplan ("Disaster Plan" in Dutch), a hardcore version of Food Not Bombs, were lined up to cook three square vegan meals a day for six weeks. Dozens of speeches and workshops were planned — from nonviolent training sessions to a class on how to climb a tree and live there, for weeks if need be, to save one of our arboreal brothers. There was an open-relationship workshop and, one of my favorites, a class on solar-powering your Walkman using the foil from a cigarette pack and a paper clip. We even had a plan for using the methane from our porta potties to power some of Rampenplan's cookers. One of the final logistical hurdles was to acquire adequate supplies of clean drinking water. For that, we needed a solar-powered water-filtration system, which, logically, required a solar generator. A big one. Luckily, Ingrid knew of one in Norway that could be donated to us. All we needed was a semitrailer and a driver to haul it to Bulgaria.

Perhaps you're aware that the distance between Norway and Bulgaria is very long. If you are not, it is about 1,700 miles. But no worries: we had the truck and the man for the job—Henerick from Freiburg, Germany, and his lorry, Hilda, a WWII-era beast covered in army green canvas that spewed black diesel smoke. I knew Henerick well—he was one of a long list of interesting activists who had spent time in Sittard—and I knew he could get the job done.

Because this was in pre-EU days, crossing borders in the former Eastern Block was, to be blunt, a bitch. The passage from Germany to Czechoslovakia alone proved to be a half-day nightmare. Czechoslovakia to Hungary required nearly another full day of arguing with officials and bribing border guards in extreme heat. Hungary to Romania was no picnic, either. But it was the border between Romania and Bulgaria that nearly did us in.

At the time, Ingrid and I were fully in love. While Henerick drove, the two of us would snuggle and make out in the cabin, and during rest stops we'd have sex any time we could—even sneaking away and screwing in treetops, precariously dangling from branches in our lust. When I wasn't humping, I was so excited about Ecotopia that I talked nonstop the entire time. Henerick must have found us annoying as hell, but he put up a good show and kept Hilda grinding along in the summer heat. After a few long days stuck at this particular border, however, our collective stress levels began to rise. The borders were ripe with prostitutes and pimps, gamblers and Gypsy thieves. Organized crime was par for the course. We would sit on the bumper of Hilda at night and watch men in pickup trucks empty a lorry-full of cigarettes and then refill it with empty boxes. We saw men wait in line for their turn at one woman hidden behind a cargo van.

At the Bulgarian border, the line hardly moved for three days. Henerick slept in the locked cab of Hilda, while Ingrid and I slept in the canvas-covered trailer with the backpacks and the generator. The heat was unbearable.

On the fourth night we learned that the ferry that transported lorries over the Danube River was broken. How long until it would be fixed, no one knew. Frustrated and restless, Ingrid and I decided to sleep on top of Hilda to get some fresh air and some great outdoor sex. Unfortunately, we weren't alone. A few hours later I climbed down to pee and saw a huge gash in the side of the truck. The generator was too big to move, but our packs—all three of them—were gone. With them went almost everything I owned, including my recently purchased prize possession—black leather pants with a patch on one ass pocket of Woodstock hugging Snoopy.

"There's some Gypsy out there," I thought, "who will never understand the meaning of such a hug."

I hesitated to wake up Henerick, who I knew was going to be pissed off beyond belief. And then there was Ingrid, sleeping in a tank top and undies that were now her only articles of clothing. That actually made me smile, but then I remembered what else was in my pack—my lithium.

Well, *fuck*.

As we sat in our underwear on the bumper of Hilda taking swigs off a bottle of Hungarian *pálinka*, we considered our options. There really was only one: get across this border and drive the remaining few hours to Ecotopia. Do this in our undies and try not to complain. Utopia needed water, after all. And eventually, we got it to them.

—※—

Ecotopia wasn't perfect, but we tried. Many among this huge group of wide-eyed hippies had their copies of Callenbach's *Ecotopia* out, believing that its central tenets were a recipe for a better future. The first order of business was to talk about our current world and how to solve its problems. Every morning while we ate our vegan breakfasts, we had a consensus-decision-making meeting. This was our template, our boots-on-the-ground action guided by the belief that dialogue could cure what ailed us. Should the camp be clothing-optional? Big discussion. What should we do about theft or illegal drugs? What about the economic inequalities between Western and Eastern participants who wanted to buy stuff at our meager eco store? Should we adhere to a common language? If so, should it be English or German? Or should we muddle through with multiple translations? These discussions, naturally, took forever and, frankly, drove me nuts. But the theory was powerful, and when it worked, it gave me a glimpse of what a utopian collective could really look like. As the days wore on, I grew more impressed with the power of such a model.

Another thing we had planned in advance for Ecotopia was a large-scale political action. This year, we were working with a local Bulgarian EYFA branch to help them raise awareness about efforts to shut down a nuclear power plant in the area. Now that the Soviet Union was kaput, many local groups were fighting for the permanent closure of the old and worn-out Soviet nuke plants. And, of course, Western companies were fighting to get the massive contracts to update them. After days of nonviolent training workshops (some of which I taught, using my Mennonite education), the camp was ready. The group was divided into four major categories: arrestables, nonarrestables, support, and logistics. Paxus, whose life's passion to this day revolves around stopping nuclear power, had me so fired up that I opted to join him in the arrestables group.

I was very nervous as I handcuffed my wrists to my neighbor activists and became part of the long human chain blocking the entrance of the nuclear power plant. To make it harder for the local police to break us apart, we had slipped our arms into long PVC pipes before locking the cuffs. So unless the cops wanted to risk cutting our hands off in front of the national Bulgarian press, we were pretty secure, or so we thought.

We chanted and sang and were feeling pretty damn proud of ourselves by the time the police came. I wondered what they could do. Cutting the pipe would be too dangerous. Beatings caught on camera would only bring us sympathy. If they tried to wait us out and let us bake in the sun for days, we had a support group ready to care for our basic needs.

Instead, the police chose a method that I had never seen before but that I have since seen and experienced many times. They pepper sprayed our eyes. And while we cried and struggled to get unlocked, they arrested us, all of us, and put us in a makeshift jail that was little more than a fenced-in field next to the actual jail.

After the cameras had been packed up and the media left, however, the police promptly released us, no questions asked. To our collective surprise, we had raised awareness, and we got to be martyrs in the process. Not bad for a day of activism.

~~~

Before our elation had worn off, and with my eyes and wrists still carrying a whiff of righteous irritation, I began walking aimlessly around the Ecotopia camp. I heard the distant sound of a violin and decided to investigate. Beyond a grove of trees, I saw a young woman sitting alone on a rock, her instrument tucked firmly under a petite chin. Her name was Litti, and she was a mischievous girl from northern Sweden. I thought she looked like a fairy and told her so. Later that day, as we walked alone in the forest, she reminded me that fairies can be very dangerous. I scoffed. She took off her clothes and ran as fast as she could into the trees. I did the same. I eventually caught her.

~~~

One evening I was smoking a joint by myself on the outskirts of camp and decided to climb a tree. I was already on a hill and figured that if I climbed high enough, I'd be able to see the entire group in the valley below. I found a solid crook to plant my foot in, wiped off my glasses, and looked down. Below me were dozens of campfires, and huddled around them were scores of like-minded folk who knew something was wrong with the world and who had decided they were going to try to make it better. There was a faint sound of singing. I knew that most of the fires were organized by language, with Bulgarians singing Bulgarian folk songs and the French singing theirs. Brits were scarce and Americans were even rarer, so there was no English-language fire. On previous nights, I had wandered between groups, sipping local hooch and listening. That was stunning enough. But as I watched from my treetop, I came up with an idea. It started with a memory of being drunk a few nights earlier with a Glaswegian named Billy Boyd, a busker who lived at EYFA's headquarters in Sittard. He noticed every campfire had one or two main guitar players. "Someone should record these folks," he had said.

I got down from the tree and found Billy. Over the next few nights we made our way to every campfire and discerned the lead musicians from each of the ethnic groups. As we talked with them, we learned that most were singing both national songs and original ones. Most of their originals had environmental themes. Our idea was this: we would create a series of CDs called Young Musicians Europe featuring environmental songs performed in native European languages by the youth of EYFA. We would build a traveling studio and tour Europe to record their songs. We would produce the first CD in time for Ecotopia next year in France and have a full-scale concert to boot. The idea caught on quickly. Everyone was fired up.

Some ideas are born in trees, others in water. Ecotopia included a lot of skinny dipping, something I'd never tried before but soon acknowledged as among the greatest of human endeavors. After our first rendezvous, Litti and I fell into a routine of making love in the morning and then going for a swim. One particular morning, after attending a dawn workshop together on praxis (the idea of putting theory in practical action), we had the idea of "theory in action" spinning in our minds and our hearts. Just as YME came into being like magic, we felt any theory could happen—we just had to dream it first. And dream we did, naked in the water.

The idea was simple but big. A peace circus. We'd find performers in EYFA, then acquire a big top, a ring, the whole nine yards. The production would move between war-torn former

Yugoslavia and Western Europe and conduct nonviolence workshops disguised as circus acts. There would be no animals but plenty of traditional circus entertainment like trapeze artists and tightrope walkers and jugglers. We would launch it next year from Ecotopia France, right after the big YME concert.

It was going to be a big year.

After our six weeks were up, Litti and I opted to take the long way back home by detouring through Turkey. Everything seemed possible now. As I shopped through bazaars and gazed at the night sky from the rooftops we slept on, I couldn't help but daydream the possibilities. Could I pull this off? Both YME and a peace circus? Raise the money, organize logistics, find the right participants, and then run them both? All in one year? I had no doubts, harbored no misgivings, and felt no fear. I wanted to change the world, by God, and this was my chance to prove it.

But embedded in all this newfound ingenuity and dreaming was a flawed logic. Because my lithium had been stolen at the Romanian border, I hadn't been taking my meds during Ecotopia. I connected this med-free hiatus with the sudden groundswell of big ideas I'd had over the past six weeks. Being off lithium had freed my genius mind. Surprisingly—and stupidly—I didn't attribute this burst of creativity to the event itself or the people I'd met and collaborated with. I never even considered that I, a young man from Ohio, might have simply been stimulated by interacting with scores of young European hippies attempting to create utopia. Instead, I vainly looked inward and diagnosed the situation accordingly. Which is a pity. Because in the coming year, the energy, ideas, and passion of others—and not my "genius"—was just what I was going to need.

A Peace Circus Burnout

Fuck you, I won't do what you tell me!
Fuck you, I won't do what you tell me!
Fuck you, I won't do what you tell me!
Motherfucker!
Uggh!

Rage Against the Machine, "Killing in the Name"

At Ecotopia, I was elected to the board of directors of EYFA. That my peers by consensus chose me to represent them was a great honor. I was relieved of my duties as editor of the *Green Tree News* so I could focus entirely on Young Musicians Europe and the Peace Circus—now the organization's two largest projects. And another thing happened at Ecotopia that, at the time, I was extremely excited about. I quit combing and washing my hair. Yes, I now had a full set of dreadlocks that stretched below my shoulders. I thought I was the coolest kid on the block.

Back in Amsterdam, my first order of business was to hunker down and raise money for my projects. By my calculations we needed around half a million dollars, which wasn't chump change, then or now. But I was determined. Grant writing became my twelve-hour-a-day job.

Paxus and I turned his flat into Grant Writing Central with computers and file cabinets and white boards everywhere. We attended workshops, read books on fund-raising, and invited development experts from organizations like World Wildlife Foundation and Greenpeace and Friends of the Earth to assist us.

We had amazing brainstorming sessions that left us exhausted but optimistic.

Most of my time was spent in the downtown Amsterdam library, which had an excellent grant research section where I studied and filled out tedious and endless applications for obscure subsets of a committee's committee in the European Community (this was before the EU, so the EC had all the money). After many long days of this kind of work, a young man needs to let off some steam. And that's where the anarchist upstairs came in. His name was Wim, and over the coming months he introduced me to a general punk lifestyle, an entirely different world of squatting, slam dancing, and speed. You may think hippies and punks are similar, but if so, you would be wrong, as I quickly discovered.

<hr>

And the truth was, Wim appeared in my life at a time when I was not merely looking for a chance to unwind from work. I was looking for a change. Or maybe an escape. Not long after Ecotopia, I realized I had let myself fall into an all-too-familiar pattern of being the savior. *Chuck will raise the money. Chuck will heal her. Chuck will take care of it. Chuck will be our leader.*

As excited as I was about the coming year, the pressure of organizing and fund-raising for Young Musicians Europe and the Peace Circus were becoming overwhelming for my twenty-two-year-old self. I was also developing a raging case of hubris. My grandiose ideas were completely unchecked; in fact, they were encouraged by the other activists. I felt like I could do no wrong, that anything I dreamed up was worth doing. Meanwhile, I was using more illegal drugs, which I now took daily. What had been a means of opening doors of perception was now becoming a crutch, something that let me escape my anxiety and that helped bolster my confidence, feeding the fantasy that anything I touched would turn to gold. Also, my decision to stop taking thorazine and to continue tinkering with my lithium doses was having a far greater effect on me that I had realized. I starting using—and not using—lithium like it was any other drug. When I needed an injection of "genius" to prepare for a couple days of brainstorming, I would quit taking it for a week or so. When I needed to hunker down and focus on my work, I reverted to my normal dosages. It was truly messing with me. And it was dangerous. There were many times when I was, simply put, psychotic and probably should have been institutionalized for the safety of myself and others. I was playing with my mental illness, treating my mania like a yo-yo on a string. I'd go days without sleep; I had a hard time telling truth from lies. I was having unsafe sex and taking way too many illegal drugs. And frankly, I was having a hard time discerning what was real. There were times when I honestly did not know whether I was tripping on acid or stone-cold sober.

I felt it happening, but rather than fight it or seek advice from others, I decided to let it ride, to see where it would take me. Pretty soon—faster than I could have imagined, actually—things got not only blurry, they got dark.

—⁓—

Paxus and I were working on yet another grant proposal in our flat when Wim busted in. He was a bald Dutchman, petite and constantly wired with real or chemically enhanced energy. He always wore overalls and a tool belt, and he carried a white five-gallon bucket filled with handyman hardware. Something in the way he carried himself suggested integrity and purity, like he was some anarchist monk of the streets. I was drawn to all of it.

Wim hung out with a group that was always on the lookout for places to squat, and after they were in, they'd try to legally claim the spot as their own. This was partly practical, as there was a serious housing crisis in Amsterdam. But there was also principle at stake: no one, for any reason, should be allowed to leave a place empty and prevent it from being useful to others. So Wim and his group would bust into these empty buildings, board up the doors and windows, and take it over. On this morning, Wim told me they'd found an abandoned bordello. The owners had been arrested, and the place had since fallen between the cracks with the authorities. It was fully stocked with booze and even had a hot tub. "Let's have a squat party!" he cried. I was fully on board.

I had been spending some of my off hours with an American I'd met. Carey was a nanny and looked like a librarian, but she was deep into S&M and edgy sex play. By this time, I'd had a lot of sex with hippies, but that was more like making love, with lots of snuggling afterward. Which was great, but no hippie I knew wanted to be spanked with a paddle until she bruised. None of my past girlfriends wanted to be tied up and whipped wearing a ball gag. Like Wim did, something in Carey opened up a new road of desire in me that I decided to follow. I figured she would love this party.

She met me outside the building in full-on fetish gear, ready for action. We drank a few anarchist snakebites (lager and cider mixed with speed) and headed for the six-person hot tub. It looked lonely, so we recruited about ten others to join us. Soon we were all naked and making out in the hot tub. Downstairs, the party was revving up: the free liquor and the intense punk music created a devil-may-care attitude that began sparking fights, chair smashing, and general wild behavior. We fed on this energy, and more naked people joined us upstairs for more of the hot tub action. As things were getting hot and heavy, there was a loud crack, and something shifted beneath us—the hot tub had broken through the ceiling joists beneath it. Suspended only by a framework of metal pipes, we screamed and sloshed about, water pouring onto the floor below. In the chaos, one naked person even fell out and plummeted to the dance floor. The rest of us hustled out, laughing and naked and unharmed. But the damage was like blood to sharks. The frenzy began. About a hundred people began ripping up the floorboards, punching through drywall, and trashing the entire house.

As the destruction ebbed, Wim and I started lighting things on fire. The flames grew out of control, and we ran off screaming into the night, sirens approaching. In a nearby alley, I stopped, slammed Carey up against a wall and sodomized her as hard as I could as I listened to the chaos and the cries of anarchy around me. I felt completely and utterly out of control. When we were done, she and I ran off into the night, looking for a new place to dance.

<center>~~~</center>

My nights were wild. But during daylight hours, I'd dust myself off and return to my projects and dreams. In particular I was intent on making progress with Young Musicians Europe. We'd cobbled together a portable recording studio, and finally Billy the busker and I were able to travel to record some of the artists chosen for the first album, which would be called *Organic Chaos*.

We began with three young Bulgarian women who had blown us away at Ecotopia with their a cappella songs. Our plan was to let the artists record whenever and wherever they wanted. Our Bulgarian friends chose well, taking us to a fourteenth-century church in a small town, a gorgeous space with great acoustics. After the equipment was set up and they'd warmed up their voices, I took a seat in a back-row pew. The stillness of the church and the beauty of their singing overwhelmed me. It was like a reminder of a past me, one I had, in many ways, forgotten, or at least smothered in drugs and alcohol and random sex. I took the time as they sang to allow myself the luxury of remembering what I had once liked about God and the church. I remembered the comfort of having Jesus in my heart.

As the women sang, a local boy climbed up the belfry and started ringing the bells in the church. The recording was seemingly ruined. But, by chance, the chimes began to synch with the rhythm of the song. The girls adapted on the fly and sang along with them. The chimes ended as their final lyrics came to a close. It was stunning. The engineer nodded at Billy, knowing they had captured a great moment on tape. I shut my eyes and, for a fleeting moment, felt connected with God's love once again.

But when I opened them again the moment was gone.

<center>~~~</center>

With *Organic Chaos* under way, I went back to organizing the much more complicated, and far less fundable, Peace Circus. I was still splitting my time between Sittard, home to the lovely Abelone, and Amsterdam and anarchy. On train rides between my two homes, I would switch the music in my Walkman. Grateful Dead for the treks to Sittard, Rage Against the Machine for Amsterdam. I was living in two worlds, and both were full of debauchery— just different kinds. Acid and Ecstasy and weed kept me going in Sittard as I organized the Peace Circus. Speed and alcohol fueled my grant writing in Amsterdam. I rarely slept, and I had sex with as many women as possible. I told myself that this formula and lifestyle was helping me achieve my goals. But that was a lie. I'd put myself on a train that was running out of track.

To this day, I am still surprised by how quickly I went from being a carefree hippie to this darker side. The obvious explanation is that I was doing too many drugs and was exhausted. But I also never rebelled as any normal teenager should. I didn't run through cornfields drinking beer, or cruise the strip, or fuck my neighbor's daughter when her parents weren't home. I think I had some pent-up rebellion looking for a home. Burning down a building was a bit much, perhaps, but again the drugs had a funny way of both amplifying everything and masking what was really going on.

Do I regret this time of my life? I had some amazingly intense experiences. Walking into an orgy and having two beautiful women's eyes light up with desire when they see you. Dancing for twenty-four hours straight. Having so much speed in your system that the world no longer speeds up but actually slows down. I wouldn't give up those moments or a thousand more like them. But now I realize that every time I received, I gave something away as well. The tabs on my tongue or the pills in my throat, the bong hits, the bottles drunk, the anonymous pussy . . . with each act a part of me was lost. And at the rate I was going, there was nowhere to go but down.

—⁓—

Around this time, Paxus had a filmmaker friend from San Francisco turn our Amsterdam flat into a production studio for an antinuke documentary about a nuclear power plant in Temelin, a small village in the Czech Republic. I offered my help as a production assistant, whatever that meant, and we all worked away. The problem was that our editor, Glynis, a redheaded forty-year-old firebrand, was a complete drunk and, at times, a distraction. And she needed to be entertained. It was, you might say, a job built for me. One day I was handed $200 and instructions not to bring her home until dawn so the others could work. Glynis and I headed straight to the red light district, feeling wild and free. We drank vodka shots and danced on more than one bar, made out with more than one patron, and did more than one line of coke. After I pulled her away from her second fight of the evening, we had found a nice, dark street corner to pace and brainstorm. It went something like this: "Let'sdosomethingcrazyman." "Yesyesyesyesyes." "Whatdowedo?" "We. Need. A victim." "A lucky bastard." "Yepaluckyone." Off we went.

In a titty bar we spied a scared looking middle-aged Danish tourist sipping a cocktail. We drew up bar stools on either side of him and began egging him on. My introduction: "If you do a double shot of rail gin, I'll let you watch my friend touch herself."

The man toyed with his drink and sputtered a bit before finally saying yes. He watched, mesmerized, as Glynis put her finger in her vagina. After that, he was our toy. We took him to the bathroom and made him touch himself in exchange for a make-out session with Glynis. He joined us for a line of coke (his first time) in exchange for some other naughtiness, and by dawn we brought his fucked-up ass back to the flat. I am pretty sure Paxus's intent by sending me away with Glynis was not to have a party show up at the flat at 5 a.m. But we didn't care. In my room, which held only a single mattress, Glynis put on a strap-on and gave that guy more memories for a lifetime. My whisky dick and dizzy head had little to offer other than encouragement, which I did loudly in the form of specific instructions. After a while, I was drawn to the large neon key, blinking in the night, advertising the key shop below. I did the last of the coke off of Glynis' ass and,

naked, crawled onto the ledge and climbed on the key. As I watched
them fuck through the window, I put a fist in air and screamed—
and I clearly remember I was sobbing, too—"Fuck you I won't do
what you tell me! Fuck you I won't do what you tell me!"

—*wm*—

In the fog of it all, *Organic Chaos* was finished and we pressed the
first CDs. Even more surprisingly, I had not only organized the first
six-month itinerary of the Peace Circus and found all the participants but also successfully raised around half a million dollars to
fund both projects. All this, in less than a year. To say I was cocky
would be putting it mildly. As one friend delicately suggested, my
hubris meter was turned up to eleven. And meanwhile, my exhaustion meter was reading twelve.

In Sittard, everyone at EYFA was busy organizing Ecotopia
France. I was working closely with the activists in charge because
the Peace Circus would launch from there and our *Organic Chaos*
benefit concert and CD launch would coincide with the final
night of Ecotopia. The logistics were a nightmare. By this time
Ingrid and Litti were in Sittard, living at EYFA and helping organize Ecotopia. Litti was an official member of the circus as well.
And Abelone was still living in Sittard, too. I was trying to maintain
a relationship with all three of them, but that was becoming a strain,
too. They were cool; I wasn't. I just didn't know what I was doing.
I was in love with all three of them, but I saw multiple relation-
ships as sexual mostly. I was missing the relationship part. I could
have used a lot more handholding walks and long talks instead
of constantly getting high and having sex all the time. And they
were reaching out too, in their own ways, because they saw my life
was falling apart. I didn't listen, of course, and, unfortunately, my
unraveling was speeding up in spectacular fashion. I desperately
needed some detox and some moments of introspection. But I
was deathly afraid of silence. Any honest reflection on God, my
mental illness, and my increasing drug problem was out of the
question. I feared stillness above all else. As if in stillness I would
be forced to look inward and find what I always feared: nothing.

With thirty days left before Ecotopia started, there were many important details and last minute fiascos to attend to. So I decided to prepare the best I could: I would take one hit of LSD every morning for the next thirty days. Why? Fair question. Part of me thinks that, deep down, I wanted to fail. Maybe I thought I was going to fail anyway, so at least everyone could blame the drugs and not me. Part of me was probably just trying to be a hard-core show-off. *I pulled it off, bitches, even when I was fucked up.* But I was so lost, so messed up, and so delusional at the time that the real reason I did it may have been even simpler. I did it for the hell of it.

Near the end of my thirty-day LSD binge I arrived exhausted and fried at Ecotopia France. Two days before Ecotopia was to start, we held EYFA's annual board meeting in a building on the same grounds. It had all the telltale signs of an activist board meeting— sleeping bags spread across the floor, roll-your-own tobacco pouches on tables, tea cups everywhere. The place smelled like patchouli and sweat. But then something clicked in my addled brain. The meeting was supposed to start later this afternoon. Why were all these people already here? Why were notes already scrawled on the white boards? Then it hit me. The meeting had started without me.

Paxus sat me down and explained what had happened. I was the first item on the agenda. All of the board members, my close friends from Sittard and around Europe, even Paxus, had spent the previous day determining my fate.

My fate, decided by consensus, didn't fare so well. After a year on the board I was removed as a member. I was also fired from EYFA and relieved of my duties as manager of the Peace Circus and executive producer of Young Musicians Europe.

I was gutted. Jesus, I thought, how can you get fired from a green anarchist youth organization that doesn't even pay you?

That you just raised five hundred grand for? A group for which you just organized, arguably, their two greatest projects ever?

The drugs and the physical exhaustion, along with the emotions I felt upon hearing Paxus's news, overtook me. I ran into the nearby woods and curled up in a ball under a tree and slept and slept.

—*m*—

I was now unemployed, had less than $100 to my name, and knew that I would lose the safety net of funding from the Brethren Voluntary Service. I also knew I was royally fucked. On-the-verge-of-a-complete-nervous-breakdown fucked. I couldn't stay at Ecotopia; I was too embarrassed. I didn't want to go back to Sittard, as so many people I knew, including Abelone, were there. Paxus told me to crash at his empty flat in Amsterdam and chill out. But while hitchhiking from southern France to Amsterdam, I was finally sober long enough to contemplate my options. Amsterdam appeared to be the most obvious short-term spot for me to land, but I also knew damn well that an unemployed and depressed Chuck in that city would yield nothing but trouble. So I took a different route.

I called Stephanie, my old girlfriend from Goshen. She was now living in Portland, Oregon, with some friends we had in common from Goshen College. She had once told me that if I ever got into some shit to call her. Well, I got into some shit. I called her. And within hours she had a ticket waiting for me in Amsterdam.

I spent the next month in Portland lying on her couch and front porch, shell shocked and numb. Every time I woke up, a sinking feeling in my stomach returned. My balloon of hubris had been popped, and now I was deflating. As its poison left my system I was faced with a pretty big question. What was next?

The idea of renting a room in Portland and working in a Grateful Dead bar scared me more than a stint in a Turkish prison. But that was probably my best option. I didn't mind leaving Europe, but not like that, not like a defeated man running from his problems. If I stayed in Oregon, it was tantamount to rolling over.

It was December 1993. The Czech Republic was about to celebrate its one-year anniversary as a new nation with the poet king, Václav Havel, as their president. I picked up one of his plays from Powell's books and didn't even finish it before my decision was made. I was moving again, my old Gypsy blood rearing up inside me. This time I was off to Bohemia.

Romantic at Last

*　　　*　　　*　　　*　　　*
　　*　　　*　　*　　　*　　*
*　　　*　　　*　　　*　　　*

Anchors Aweigh

Twenty-five whores in the room next door.
Twenty-five floors and I need more.
I'm looking for the can in the candy store
And colors I ain't seen before.
                                        Sisters of Mercy, "Vision Thing"

Once my decision was made, I saw fleeting glimpses of an old friend: optimism. I was down but not out. Some self-discipline was called for. I began biking a lot in Portland, adding muscle to my puny thighs. I stayed off illegal drugs except for some weed now and then to dampen, albeit temporarily, my mania and the voices. I also abstained from sex for the month and even read a few novels. I didn't, unfortunately, do a lot of self-reflection. Because I was still tinkering with my lithium and taking no other prescribed medications, my mind would often race, even when I was sitting quietly on a porch, watching the sunset. I would breathe deeply, trying to slow everything down.

And then there I was again, crossing the Atlantic. On the plane ride, I felt a familiar sense of peace and purpose. I felt I would be just fine, that my life was back under control—that I could change the world.

But on my first day in Prague I found the Roxy.

The Roxy is the coolest fucking club. Ever. It's this huge, brutish bunker of concrete with caverns leading nowhere and somewhere at the same time. It was where Charter 77 was started, Václav Havel's organization that helped overthrow the Soviet Union. It reeked of the Velvet Revolution and Sparta cigarettes.

When I arrived it was a packed, drugged-out scene. The DJ was blasting techno, and an old, familiar impulse quickly overcame my recent well-intentioned abstinence—my blood was simmering with it, the urge to party was damn near irrepressible. And beyond that, and with apologies to Abba, there was something in the air that night. It was the early 1990s in Prague. This was the capital of Bohemia. At the time, I didn't even know what that meant, but one look around at the Roxy and I was like, "Yes, I want to fucking roll in here, right now." To do otherwise—to stay sober, my feet planted on terra firma—seemed like an insult to what the Fates were presenting me. I'd messed up before. But a guy can learn from his mistakes, right? This time around, I'd get it right.

No matter the country, buying illegal drugs is usually a nightmare. There's the rigamarole of talking in code as you look for the dealer, and as you inch closer to "the man," you must prove you're not a narc to everyone you encounter. Once you find said dealer the charade continues, even in a crowded club where the people around you are actually *doing* drugs. In the process of doing all this in the Roxy, I picked up an Australian, a Brit, and a very energetic Czech teenager who, like me, were all looking for Ecstasy. After the charade was done, I'd secured us one pill. One pill! That's all we could afford.

As we looked at that little pill cut into four even smaller pieces, our sadness was palpable. A quarter of a pill would do basically nothing and we all knew it. Meanwhile, the dance floor and those strobes were calling us like Sirens and I wasn't tied to shit.

Then the Australian says, "I heard that if you take coffee as an enema you get a stronger effect. Janet Jackson was addicted to it." Goddammit, he was proposing we all do Ecstasy enemas. I liked his logic. It was time to stick that fourth of a pill up my ass. Fuck it.

After we finished our business, we hit the dance floor. I'd taken a lot of Ecstasy by that point—this wasn't like taking Ecstasy; this was like being hit by a ton of happy bricks. The psychoactive mood-altering Drano flushed out my worries and cares. MDMA,3,4, methylenedioxymethamphetamine here I come. Boombabyboombabyboom!

I got a beer and leaned back in a corner of the dance floor, right by one of the speakers, and sat there trippin' away.

There was this woman.

She had short hair—only three or four inches long—but at the bottom of it she'd braided in strips of carpeting. She was Czech and had the body of a model and was wearing some kind of Victorian-era corseted dress, along with combat boots and a thick chainmail necklace. "13" was tattooed on her belly. Her dark eyes shone from a face covered in white makeup. She was smoking a bindi. She pointed at me. I'm thinking, *It's Medusa! Run for your life!* But I couldn't move.

She danced over to me and kissed me on the mouth. I may have been fucked up, but I knew this kiss was a test. Of what, I didn't know, but it was a test.

I didn't turn to stone. And to confirm that fact, she reached her hand down my pants.

I don't move, I don't touch her. People are dancing near us and I'm kind of doing this leaning-sitting thing. She then proceeds to pull my pants down to just above my knees in one aggressive tug. She pushes my chest and slams me against the wall then hikes up the Victorian dress and fucks me—hard.

Or, more accurately, she straddles me in this really weird, impossible angle. I'm trying to hold my butt up with my hands but keep slipping. Her one hand is still on my chest full force, and the other one is grabbing me by the jawbone. I was scared. I was in love. After what felt like a month but was probably more like three minutes, she digs her boots into my calves, throttles my neck, and lifts her head back and screams. And then she steps away and starts to leave. She must have taken pity on the puppy dog "Do I get to come now?" look on my face, not to mention my hard-on-with-my-pants-down-to-my-knees-on-a-crowded-dance-floor posture. So she slowly dances back to me, licks her long finger-nailed index finger and jams it up my ass.

Except for the pill I'd rammed up my butt twenty minutes earlier, I had never had anybody or anything up my ass before. And that Ecstasy enema had made my asshole very sensitive. While I'm processing all this, she clamps down hard on my cock with her other hand. Not in a nice way—she just squeezes it like a vice grip. I might have shrieked. Meanwhile, the fingernail on her other hand hits my prostate and she looks at me and says "vroom" and then pulls her hands away. I came, just like that.

And then this corseted ghost is standing there with my cum on her hands. She looks at me and backs up, dancing and licking it off. And in a strobe-light moment she disappeared into the dance floor. I'm thinking: I'm in the coolest place in the world in the coolest moment of my life. I don't have a place to live. I don't have a job. I don't have any money. I don't know anybody. I'm no longer interested in trying to change the world, and I'm not sure I believe in anything at all. I'm right where I wanted to be. I was finally, truly adrift, cock out and fucked up and free.

———

The next morning, I adjusted my weight on the couch cushions I'd fashioned into a bed the previous night and peeked out of my sleeping bag. The squat where I was crashing had no heat, electricity, or running water. I could have used all three at that moment. I could have used many things—some aspirin and coffee for starters. I lit a cigarette and surveyed my situation. I was fucked. I was lonely. I was cold. My asshole hurt. God was gone. My circus was on tour without me. I had about two weeks worth of money, if I was frugal. My post-Ecstasy crash was telling me to hide somewhere and cry. The otherworldly enchantment of the Roxy was fading, and in its place was a new wellspring of doubt. If there was a reason I'd come to Prague, I'd forgotten what it was.

I was huddling deeper inside my sleeping bag, bracing for a few hours of self-pity and anxiety, when I heard the sound. It was faint but clear. Music. I got up to find its source.

The squat comprised four, four-story buildings situated in a square with a central courtyard. Each of the buildings' four entrances were booby-trapped against neo-Nazis and other fascist groups. Unlike in Paris or Amsterdam, squatters in Eastern Europe didn't fear the police—there was nothing a little bribe couldn't cure. Rather, the fear was you'd wake up to some right-winger in jackboots hitting you upside the head with a pipe.

I unzipped my bag, got up, and carefully sidestepped some pretty ingenious traps and weaponry. I walked down a hallway, following the sound until I found what I was looking for. In an empty room with dusty wood floors, seated in front of a fire with her back to me, was a young woman sporting a Dead Kennedys leather jacket and pink Mohawk. She was practicing violin. Near the door, I quietly sat down so as not to disturb her and listened.

Soon, my cloudy musings from moments ago cleared up. The defeated, hungover, and possibly unhinged man who had been prepared to hunker down for a long and cold winter of misery in a squat in Prague once again surveyed his situation. I shut my eyes and listened to this young Czech punk playing classical music. Only a few years ago, she would have been in the streets, participating in the nonviolent marvel that punctuated the end of one of the great evils of the twentieth century.

It dawned on me that I had met this woman before. She was an antinuke activist. Her name was Sarka.

A short tram ride from where I was sitting in Prague's sixth district, there was a nature preserve called Divoka Sarka (Wild Sarka), named after one of the coolest female warriors I have ever heard of. As legend has it, the lands around Prague some fifteen hundred years ago were the site of a civil war between the genders. On one side of the Vltava River the women sought to maintain a matriarchal society; on the other, a large male tribe, ruling from Vysehrad, made its bid for power. The women knew they were outnumbered, but the brave and beautiful young Sarka devised a plan. Using herself as bait, she devised a way to woo and capture the men's best warrior, Ctirad. Her plan worked, and Ctirad was captured and killed. But the women were ultimately defeated, as the men avenged Ctirad's death. Rather than surrendering, Sarka threw herself off a cliff (now called Divci Skok or "Girls' Jump") in an act of defiance. Her body was never found.

Her body was never found. Yet here she sits, a defiant punk rocker playing violin.

I got up and walked over to her. We shared my cigarettes and the chicken she was roasting over the fire. It started to snow through the open window as she resumed her music. I shut my eyes, leaned my head back, and felt the flakes melt on my face.

They say Prague is magic. I don't know if I believe in magic or not, but I felt it that day.

"There are still a few men who love desperately," as JD Salinger said. It's a sentimental phrase, a romantic idea, and it hits on a central question I've yet to shake. Why can't you believe in garden gnomes instead of God? Being a sentimental dreamer doesn't mean you have to be a part of a movement or a mission. This is who I was at this moment and probably for the rest of my life. A helpless romantic.

I may have been alone, but after that morning, I was sure I wouldn't be for long.

Joy's Corduroys versus
the Mutoid Waste Company

Sunday morning I'm waking up.
Can't even focus on a coffee cup.
Don't even know who's bed I'm in.
Where do I start, where do I begin.
Chemical Brothers, "Where Do I Begin"

In Prague in the 1990s, every expat conversation began with the same question. "Hey, where do you live?" Nobody could find a place because there was no economy for renting under Communism, and when I got to Prague there still wasn't. Plus, by the time I arrived in early 1994, thousands of foreigners were already there. Young people from across Europe—French and Italians, Danes and Dutch—had flocked to the geographic and nascent cultural center of the continent. The biggest group of all was the Americans. We were everywhere. As the *Los Angeles Times* wrote in January 1992,

> Ten thousand Americans in Czechoslovakia—many of them twentysomethings—is the hip-pocket estimate, although no one, not even the Czechoslovak immigration department, knows for sure. It seems to have happened overnight—and in fact may be just beginning. There was Paris in the '20s; will it be Prague in the '90s?

Add the young Czechs pouring in from the countryside, and the city just exploded, which was awesome! Unless you wanted somewhere to live.

One of the best antidotes to homelessness, as I learned after my first night after the Roxy, was to squat. So I did just that. I took up residence in a three-hundred-year-old apartment building with a bunch of hard-core Czech anarchists, which was fun for someone like me, who had a history of idolizing those who dressed in black, shaved their heads, and were generally bad ass. Of course, this casual, unstable living situation brought with it myriad hassles, occasional dangers, and serious discomfort in the winter. But those were burdens I could bear. The reward was that I could see the Vltava through the cracks in my boarded up windows. I could walk via Karlův Most to Staroměstské Náměstí. I could drink twenty-cent beers and chain-smoke Spartas. I read Kafka or Kundera or Hrabal by candlelight and stirred noodles on my one-burner gas stove, and I wrote a lot of bad poetry. I spent many evenings alone, too. And when I was alone, I often thought of how I'd gotten here. My years as a dogmatic believer—in Jesus, in the environmental movement—all seemed like a waste. So often I had approached life as an open vessel, floating in space, waiting with great anticipation for the next big thing to come fill me up. I'd had some awesome experiences, and here I was lucking out again by hitting Prague in its newfound prime. But for what seemed like for the first time in my life, I just wanted to float. I wasn't looking for anything to sink my teeth into. I just wanted . . . nothing.

That first winter I hung around a lot at the Globe, an American coffee shop and bookstore near my squat. I didn't have running water, so the management took pity on me and let me wash up in their sinks, brush my teeth, and use the bathroom in the mornings.

One winter morning after a refreshing sponge bath, I grabbed a cup of coffee and struck up a conversation with this woman who looked like she was in her mid-sixties. Her accent was American, but she didn't look it. Americans "fresh off the boat" were easy to spot, their skin ruddy and, well, healthy. They hadn't yet been afflicted by the white vegetables of a Prague winter, the alcohol abuse, the chain-smoking, or the low-quality brown "coal," a heating source somewhere between peat and lignite that made your boogers hard and black and covered your teeth in grit. This woman, though, she looked Czech.

"Are you an American?" I asked.

"No. I'm Czech. I live here."

In reality, she was a bit of both. She was born and raised in America, but as a Communist activist during the Red Scare in the 1950s, she decided to get out. Thanks to her Czech ethnicity, she was able to emigrate to Czechoslovakia, where she began working for the Communist Party and the Soviets. Because she was an American Communist, they, of course, welcomed her with open arms, and she became a leader in the Czech Communist Party.

Her name was Joy. She told me how she fell in love with another party member and started a family in Prague. All was well until the fall of the Berlin Wall, the Velvet Revolution, and the end of the Soviet Union. Now, in the early 1990s, prospects were dim for a Communist in Prague. So Joy was planning a return trip to the United States to visit relatives she hadn't seen in four decades.

Her plan was to return for a year, during which time she'd need someone to flat sit for her. She described her place—a two-bedroom, luxury penthouse apartment with a piano and a library and bar. It sounded beautiful. By the time we finished our coffee we agreed that I would look after her flat for that year. No more squatting. No more looking. I was elated.

Within a month, as my own Prague Spring was arriving, I moved my army duffle bag into my new digs. I sublet the extra room out for foreign hard currency—Czech crowns were worthless outside the country's borders at the time—to Erika, a hot, cynical, whip-smart American woman who had just moved to Prague from Missouri with a one-way plane ticket and a philosophy degree in her pocket.

I eventually dubbed the place "Joy's Corduroys" because the closets were full of corduroy pants that fit us both. We'd wear Joy's pants and play her piano. We found her stash of scotch and drank it. She had expensive art on the walls and many Western comforts like hot running water. It wasn't long before word got out and friends were crashing on our couches. The flat became a haven for sex, drugs, heavy drinking, live music, and philosophical arguments late into the night. It was heaven.

On our first night at Joy's, Erika and I made a home cooked meal and drank multiple bottles of Czech wine to celebrate our fortunes. One thing led to another, as they often do for free-spirited drunk twenty-somethings, and we ended up in the master bedroom, naked and kissing. We rolled around on the bed, and Erika ended up on top of me. As she reached down to put me inside her I paused and said, in all sincerity, "Promise not to fall in love with me." She responded, like any sane and intelligent person would, by laughing. She took a moment to compose herself and then, with a head shake, said, "Ok, promise not to fall in love with me." We shook hands to seal the deal. Neither one of us knew at the time that, twenty years later, she would still be shaking her head at me.

By day, I would tour the city and its environs. I played a lot of chess and enjoyed Prague's many free classical music concerts. I started working, too; my experience from working with EYFA and on the *Green Tree News* helped me land the first in a string of odd jobs for activist groups. But early on, working was not my focus. I just wanted to breathe in all that Prague magic.

—mm—

After a few months, my solitude had come to an end. I quickly made friends, for better or worse. One of my best—both then and to this day—was Heath.

One day, while Erika was away visiting her boyfriend in England, Heath brought me good tidings.

"Hey man, there's this party coming up. This one's the real thing."

Coming from Heath, this meant something. A former Army tank driver from Wisconsin, he was a DJ who already had a few prison-looking tattoos when I met him, along with a crooked nose, the result of a broken nose that never got set right. He was also a heavy and broody drinker. It might not sound like much, but the way Heath carried himself proved attractive to just about everyone. He dated a string of what looked like Czech supermodels, and within our crowd in Prague, he quickly became our moral compass. If Heath didn't approve of some business deal you were about to make or deemed that club "a fucking sell-out place, man," it had great influence. He knew himself well, while the rest of us mostly didn't. I recognized in Heath someone who could steer me right. He knew what it was like to put water on your cereal. He understood loss.

He was also a guy who knew where to find the real parties.

So when he tells me about the Spiral Tribe, a group of twenty-three DJs who will be joined by the Mutoid Waste Company for an epic techno party, I'm all ears. Before he starts talking about beats per minute and 808 drum machines and strobe systems, I cut him off.

"You had me at 'twenty-three.' I'm in."

Within days, the rave was being billed across town as the event of the year.

By coincidence, my Czech co-worker at the time asked if I could help her friend get some of her mates into the country—some band or something, she told me. At the time, she and I were serving as freelance consultants for a side project, coordinating the antinuclear Walk Across Europe event, and my role required me to spend a lot of time coordinating visas and border crossings. Her language skills and our office equipment (including a coveted fax machine) meant that we were often asked to assist with such things.

Naturally, I said yes. All I needed was a list of everything they were bringing in—band gear, stage equipment, trucks, cars—plus a photocopy of each person's passport.

A couple days later I received a huge fax. Reading over their equipment list, it dawns on me. It's them—the Spiral Tribe and the Mutoid Waste Company! The list started simply enough with amps and lights and drum kits. But then came the dune buggies and twenty-foot robots and flamethrowers and cannons and even a painted tank (dubbed "the Pink Panzer"). The final item: "one Russian MiG 21 fighter aircraft."

It seems crazy today, but this crew and their gear made it through the border without any problems (accompanied by a padded envelope of deutsche marks), par for the course for Eastern Europe in the early 1990s. After seeing the list, I knew I would not miss this fucking party for the world.

〜〜〜

On my first crossing of the Atlantic, I had given up thorazine. Now, a few short years later, I wanted to give up lithium. Something clicked when I saw a fighter jet on the list of items Spiral Tribe was bringing in. The time had come to unblock my dopamine D_2 receptors in my brain. To bring back the voices. To admit more loose associations. Give me the nonfunctional mood swings. Give me sinks to hide under. See you later my nemesis, lithium. For years, you came twice daily and in large doses. But not anymore.

This would be a more complicated decision for me today, but back then, it was simple. I was tired of the constant reminder of what was wrong with me. I looked at those pills twice a day for years, and every time I had a mini-existential crisis. Was I "a hero with a thousand faces" or just another zombie on soma controlled by the man?

By this point in my life, lithium had done its job. It had made my ups and occasional downs less up and downy. But I really missed those wild ups—the crackling energy, the limitless to-do lists conquered, the sexual energy, the bold ideas bubbling from my guts that always seemed doable. It was exciting to be manic. I had my own internal drug, waiting to be unleashed, and yet I kept stuffing it back in its cage.

Part of me feared what would happen to me without the lithium. My tinkering with self-medication had blown up in my face before. But experience is the ultimate teacher. I would know better this time. Fear was no excuse. What was I waiting for?

Today, I know more about mania's dark side, the long-term effects that accrue from lack of sleep or the near constant flow of adrenaline. I know that while manic, I always talk but rarely listen. It decimates empathy while exalting selfishness. It strains friendships and can rain hell on those who love you.

But back then, I didn't consider those things. I only thought of how much I could gain, of the powers I'd kept bottled up for too long.

Thus I decided, once again without telling a soul, that the rave would be my no-meds coming out party.

I prepared meticulously. With a half-life of twenty-four hours, lithium took about four to five days to leave my system. Then the tsunami of mania would hit the shore. The party was set to start on Friday night. I flushed my meds at midnight on Monday. I watched them swirl down the toilet and into the sewer and thought: here comes my swan dive. This shaman is about to go into the deep end.

For better, and for worse, it would be fifteen years before I took another psychiatric medication.

—*mm*—

The rave was about four hours by car from Prague, somewhere near Poland in the foothills of the Tatra Mountains. There was no exact address and the starting time was vague. Posters went up and came down. Bits of information passed around, rumors spread; it was all part of the game. But as carloads of excited Czech teens passed us on back roads, we knew we were on the right trail. And when we saw in the distance a MiG fighter converted into a DJ booth, its fuselage and wings ablaze with directional running lights, we knew our forty years of wandering the wilderness were over. We had found the Promised Land.

The scene was part Mad Max, part Monty Python, and part Wizard of Oz. You could say it was beautiful—some trees here and there and a view of the mountains. But it was just a field, really, sun baked and dusty. Perfect for forty-eight hours of debauchery.

The Pink Panzer was there, as were fire-breathers walking on massive, metal stilts. Men in suits of armor rode twenty-foot-long motorcycles outfitted with rear wheels of spiked steel that tore up the earth. Broken-down cars had been customized into postmodern sculptures that we crawled into and out of while listening to sounds from space through gas masks someone had fashioned into headphones. A rubber-clad woman held reins attached to the neck of a naked man on all fours, replete with a saddle and butt plug ponytail, and handed out Noxzema and surgical masks. A twenty-foot manned robot made nitrous oxide balloon animals for the crowds. Others worked on grotesque sculptures made from what looked like roadkill. Exercise bikes were hooked up to strobe lights. There was a working elevator to nowhere. It was ground zero in a post-apocalypse Europe.

After soaking it all in, Heath and I set off to find the Spiral Tribe. We ran into some guy in a WWII helmet. He had a wrench in his back pocket and was elbow deep in a nonfunctioning generator. We asked if he knew where the tribe was. In reply, he took off his hat, revealing the number "23" tattooed over and over again in a crown around his bald head—the symbol of the Spiral Tribe. We struck up a conversation, and though we only understood about 10 percent of what he said owing to his heavy Glaswegian accent, he soon gathered that we were the Americans who helped them with their visas. This made him very happy. He says, "Am ferrin' oot fur a bevvy." We made him repeat himself three times before we realized he was offering us a drink. We accepted, of course. Then, in a fake high British accent, he yells, "Bring out the punch!"

From seemingly nowhere (but most likely from one of several black canvas-covered trucks nearby) two women emerged—each tattooed and dotted with curious scabs, their heads half dread-locked, half shaved. They were carrying a small blanket together. They unfolded it slowly to reveal a water bottle wrapped in black electrical tape with an orange 23 written on it. They lifted their cargo with reverence, and others soon gathered around, blowing their mouths like horns. The ceremony of it was awesome; Heath and I were delighted.

In retrospect, I realize I should have thought, "Find out what's in that bottle, Chuck." But I was too ready to take things to the next level, whatever that meant. They asked us to kneel to receive the elixir, and with the sound of tools banging on metal echoing in our little valley, I grabbed the bottle, tilted my head, and drank.

I handed the bottle to Heath and he, too, drank deeply. We stood, and the small congregation formed a line in front of us. One by one, they moved forward and punched each of us in the arm. Smack! Smack! Smack! Twenty-three people, twenty-three punches. The last one yells, "You been punched!"

There was a young woman watching the ceremony in a detached way. She was petting a mangy dog and weaving some sort of walking stick out of wires. She looked at us with pity. The punch, she told us, may or may not have contained the following: methamphetamine, lysergic acid diethylamide, MDMA, and methadone. And probably some vitamin C. All shaken (not stirred) with an Everclear du jour.

Heath and I look at the MiG fighter and then at one another.

"What are we going to do?" I say.

"Dude, we're going to ride it out. It's going to be a tough time. There's nothing we can do about it."

It wasn't long before the meth was pumping through my veins. It acted as an accelerator for the other drugs, and they crashed into me over and over again. Soon I grew short of breath. I began to see things. I'm sweating. I'm confused. My heart beats too fast and then way too slow. I get paranoid. I fall in love, deeply. I can't think clearly, then I can think of everything all at once. I find beauty but I can't find my cigarettes. I itch. And in between it all I dance. The music is thumping now, and it accelerates through the towers of speakers and bounces off the Tatras and I dance my fucking ass off, because in the rain in that field in post–Communist Eastern Europe, full of far too many illegal drugs and not enough legal ones, I am—and I feel this viscerally, repeatedly, and in a variety of dimensions—free.

But at some point, as it always does, the music ends.

It's mid-morning, maybe 11 o'clock. A few stragglers keep dancing to the sounds of gas-powered generators, but most people are back in their tents. They'd taken acid or Ecstasy, and now they're chilling because it's a two-day party, after all, and this is the end of day one. The punch, however, has taken away our option of chilling. We're fucking fucked up.

We shuffle about, past the snoring, farting tents, when Heath notices we've arrived at the main stage. Much of the equipment is still there, including a drum set and an electric guitar.

"Could you figure out how to plug those into the main system?" I ask.

"Fuck yeah."

We plug in. I settle in at the drums and go ape shit. Heath's creating feedback loops with the amps. We are, suddenly, rock stars at an epic level, until, that is, several people grab us and tell us to stop. One of them says, "I'm going to fucking kill you if you don't get off the stage." We crack up, but eventually, we do as we're told.

And then things turned more hazy and much less funny. I lost Heath somewhere. I found a tree to sit against and just breathed in and breathed out. The intensity of the punch wouldn't stop. I wanted it to stop.

Some guy comes up to me and asks, "Are you all right?" I can't speak.

"This will help," and he hands me some alien object and walks away. My brain said drink, and I did. It was a pint of peach vodka. I'm trying not to cry or fall apart. My heart is palpitating. I'm tripping balls. It's noon now, and the sun is high and hot, but the shit I'm seeing is dark and bad. So I drink.

And that's when these two Brits walk up. They are the meathead asshole types you picture overturning a car after a soccer match. They looked as though they'd been drinking all night and wanted a fight. Back in my anti-fa days in Amsterdam, we called them "snakebites," after our favorite drink.

They start in. "You're one of the guys putting fucked-up music on the stage, aren't you?" "Don't American mums teach their boys respect or were they too busy shaggin'?" That sort of thing. Again, I say nothing. Talking still wasn't an option.

"The fuck's wrong with you? Fucking wanker." Whatever. They're pissed. They wouldn't leave.

At the time I had a goatee about eight inches long that I tied off with a little rubber band at the bottom, like a really, really stupid ponytail. One of them says, "I don't like your goatee."

Finally, my misfiring neurons allowed me to speak. "Go away." I pleaded. "Please go away." It was like red meat to lions.

"Whatch you think? Do you like this motherfucker's beard?"

"It's a disgoosting American wanker beard."

"I don't like it either. Should we cut it off?"

"All right. Put your feet on his chest, and I'll cut it off this asshole."

Out comes a blade. It was probably little more than a Swiss Army knife, but at the time it seemed like a serial killer's ax to me. Would they really do this? I was so fucked up, and their aggression was like a whole other presence, a fourth person looking to do harm. I wanted it all to disappear. I could have reasoned with them, but instead, with one combat-footed boot planted in the ground beneath me, I kicked my other foot up in an awkward attempt to shoo them away. I aimed it at the man with the knife. My boot hit the knife, jamming the blade through his other hand, right through the meat between the thumb and index finger—thunk.

He falls to his knees and begins screaming. Blood is soon dripping down his forearm and off his elbow. His friend begins to yell, too, hollering "What the fuck!?" over and over.

They panic, and because I am a drugged-out sponge of other people's emotions at the moment, I panic, too. And although I'm seeing things that are not there and not really understanding what's happening, I do remember staring at the bloody knife on the dusty ground.

It doesn't take long for their shock to transform into anger. The wounded man turns on me, slams his knees on my chest, and starts to shove his bloody hand in my mouth. He shouts, "Welcome to AIDS, motherfucker!" and with his other hand repeatedly punches me in the forehead.

That's when the African American torch song leader of gay Bohemia comes to my rescue. Curtis, a boy from Alabama who had become the party diva of Prague, is celebrating his fortieth birthday. His six-foot-three frame is stunning in a wedding dress, the train carried by two beautiful Czech boys-in-waiting. The front of the dress is cut away, exposing his infamous thirteen-inch cock.

Curtis comes over to me and says, "Darling, we're leaving now." He grabs my arm and pulls me up and away, and just like that, I'm extracted. He and his party lead me to his car. They all squeeze in front while I sit alone in the back seat.

We drive the four hours back to Prague. No one says anything to me. They offer me a cigarette every so often and I smoke. Eventually I start to convulse and dry heave. They would pull over and wait for me by the side of the car. They would give me water while I paced, trying to get my shit together, then we would drive again until the heaving returned.

My guardian angels dropped me off at my apartment building. There was a note on my door. In English it read, "You're out. I need you out Monday." It was signed by Joy's cousin, who lived in Prague. It was Saturday.

As I walked into the apartment, two recent memories converged. The first was from the rave. There had been a storm, a really bad storm that knocked out the electricity and left us all tripping balls in a dark, quiet field, soaking wet. The second memory was my decision to leave the windows open in the flat before I left for the rave. Thirteen floors up, all the fresh air would be a perfect welcome, I'd thought, for Erika when she returned home Monday from England.

The wind and rain had blasted through the flat like a hurricane. A balcony window was broken. There was broken art and glass on the floor. Brown water stains peppered the perimeters.

I didn't think of the man I stabbed or his claim that he was going to give me AIDS (he didn't, thankfully). I didn't think of my lovely-and-about-to-be-very-pissed-off roommate. I didn't think of Joy and how I'd pissed on her generosity. I didn't think about Heath or the party or even try to conjure some sweet childhood memory that could bring me solace. I just went over to the couch, swept off some broken glass with my hand, clutched a nearby blanket, and cried myself to sleep—dreaming of little pale red lithium birds, flying effortlessly in a straight line, singing ever so sweetly. Off in the distance another storm was brewing over the mountains and heading my way, its prevailing winds could be heard over the patter of those old, familiar voices saying "Chuck? Chuck? Chuck? Chuck? Chuck? Chuck? Chuck?"

—*mm*—

That party was a mistake. Ditching my lithium and pumping myself with a cocktail of mind-bending illegal drugs could have killed me. I shouldn't have done it. But that's me talking now—the middle-aged me. There has been a lot of honest blood, sweat, and tears shed since that night on the couch. I look back at that young man, alone and scared, and it breaks my heart. I will deny no one their path—including me. But if I had to do it all over again I would not have stopped taking those meds. Any of them. I wasted a lot of years in my twenties, experiencing unnecessary suffering from my mental illness. And, frankly, I'm lucky—and grateful—that I even survived long enough to write these words.

But that was then and this is now. I'm sorry, young me. I wish I could have helped you, for you are going to need it. If I could, I'd give you this advice, and ask you to heed it well: know thyself. Let that be your law.

Eureka: Construction Dust, Novella 1 in Homage to the Mrs.

You, soft and only,
You, lost and lonely,
You, strange as angels,
Dancing in the deepest oceans,
Twisting in the water.
You're just like a dream.

The Cure, "Just Like Heaven"

Years (and many flats) later, Erika and I found a one-room apartment above the coal yard of a train station in Prague. As I watched the trains go in and out, I was inspired: God, how I wanted Erika to see Amsterdam. But God, were we broke, too broke, even, for the trains. Erika had a grand total of $250 in "rainy day" savings. And me, I had nothing. Except, of course, a plan.

Paxus and one of his lovers, Clara, had agreed to essentially swap flats with us. For three weeks, they'd stay in our place in Prague and we'd move to his in Amsterdam. Hitchhiking would be our mode of transportation. Broke or not, we'd at least be in Amsterdam—it was our first vacation together, and I wanted it to be memorable.

Erika had never hitchhiked before, but by this point I considered myself an expert and bragged about it to her all the time.

Not only had I made it from Ohio to San Francisco as a teenager, but I hitchhiked to EYFA meetings across Europe for years as well. As we daydreamed about those three weeks together in Amsterdam, Erika came up with a brilliant idea. When we arrived, why not spend her rainy day fund on something special, just for her? Specifically, a labia piercing. This was our new mission. We were ready.

—ⵡⵡ—

After weeks of daydreaming and planning, one cold November night we took a short midnight train from Prague to Brno on the German border. Paxus had told us about a line of abandoned train cars at the Brno station where we could spend the night, so with sleeping bags in hand we headed straight for them, already thinking ahead to dawn, when, at the border, we'd stick our thumbs out and really start our hitchhiking journey.

Unfortunately, we apparently weren't the first cheapskates to try mooching the free lodging, because all the cars were now locked. It was snowing hard, and after a long argument—not our first on this trip, nor would it be our last—we opted to make the short walk to the border right then and see if we could get lucky and snag a ride. But after an hour of shivering failure, that plan failed, too. More arguing ensued until we reluctantly decided that a nearby construction site was as good a spot as any to grab a few hours of sleep. The site was covered in what we thought was a light snow that must have blown in from the unfinished sides, and with a sense of adventure we threw our bags down, hunkered inside them, and tried to laugh about our palatial "shelter."

Somehow we fell asleep. At dawn we were rousted by construction workers starting their shift. A few of them stared at us like we were freaks, which was to be expected, I suppose. But then we noticed what was going on: the floors we had slept on were not covered with snow but a thin layer of construction dust. And we were covered. Our sleeping bags, packs, clothes and even our hair had turned white. We looked each other over and laughed. We didn't even fight about it, we just packed up and left.

As we walked, I jabbered on and on about whatever came to mind. This is what I do in the mornings—just free-associate, sentence into paragraph, one story melding into the next observation. Erika, needing a cup of coffee and a cigarette, just sighed.

Perhaps mistaking her silence for weariness, I broached the subject of her $250 for the first time.

"Let's just buy two tickets from Brno to Amsterdam," I suggested. Even before she said no, the look in her eyes conveyed a simple question: What kind of man tries to spend his girl's labia-piercing money?

Unbeknownst to us, we were now in the middle of one of the worst snowstorms this part of Europe had seen in decades. We sat at the border for hours until someone finally picked us up, a single man with dirty skin and clothes, his long finger nails filed into points, a German metal band hammering out strange music from his speakers. "A creeper," as Erika would put it. He promised to take us to a rest stop at the Autobahn—a perfect place to hitchhike—though he needed to make a quick stop at his house first. That seemed odd, but we were desperate. At his house, we waited in the car, shivering, until he returned and wordlessly fired up the engine. He drove us for a while longer but suddenly changed his mind. Amid a full-on blizzard, he stopped on the side of a random road and told us to get out.

Our next ride was a U.S. military vehicle that took us in the opposite direction to a Burger King on an American military base. As we sipped a cup of fast-food joe, we took stock of the situation. We were basically twenty miles from the Czech border, nowhere near the Autobahn, and about to be stranded, because, as the young soldier told us, "They're closing the roads due to the storm any minute now."

Cautiously, I broached the subject for the second time. Erika's cash could get us to Amsterdam in a few hours. I figured her image of me as the Great Hitchhiker was already shot, so I went for broke. "I am sure it will not cost all of the $250 to get us both to Amsterdam from here via train. The rest of the money can go for the piercing. Maybe get a cheaper piercing?"

Again, the look: What kind of man tries to get his girl a discount vagina piercing? With the moxie I've always admired in her, she convinced me that we needed to get clever and soldier on. So we did. Literally. With a little coaxing that bordered on begging, we convinced a soldier to drive us in his camouflaged Hummer to the Autobahn. From there we made it to Amsterdam in no time.

—*wm*—

The blinking yellow key from my not-so-distant past never looked so good. In our time at Paxus's flat, we had a blast smoking all my old friends' weed, visiting museums, going to food markets, and walking along all the canals. We ate a lot of bread and cheese with the little money we had but we were happy. And, shockingly, we'd spent only the tiniest fraction of Erika's labia-piercing money. We scouted out several piercing shops before Erika finally found the one she liked just a day before we were to leave. She walked right in, plunked her money down and sauntered into a back room with a guy covered in piercings and tattoos. I waited in the lobby and made the mistake of picking up an album of surprisingly detailed photos showing the step-by-step processes of a variety of penis piercings. That alone made me woozy and required me to ask the freak lady behind the counter for some cold water. As I started to recover Erika emerged, glowing from her experience. My wooziness faded. I couldn't even see the piercing but I found the woman in front of me to be the sexiest beast alive.

—*wm*—

After our first hitchhiking fiasco, we'd smartened up enough to check the weather before we began our return home. We also made a more exact plan, replete with a map. Our first ride took us from Amsterdam to Berlin. We figured Berlin to Prague would be a breeze.

Within minutes, we met some Polish guy and accepted a ride in his warm, cozy van. Because it was getting late and we were both road weary, we soon fell asleep. I slept soundly, blissfully confident that my broken German and our collective broken Czech had been close enough to Polish to inform the man we were headed to Prague. Nope. We woke up hours later in northern Poland, in a town that kind of sounded like "Praha."

Erika looked at me and spoke some pretty honest words. "Chuck, my pussy really hurts, and I want to go home."

So we caught a ride—some of us more bow-legged than others—to the nearest train station and found, to our surprise, that one of those trans-European express trains with showers and plush seats that fold *all* the way back was leaving in one hour for Prague. Of course, we had no money left, but we were desperate. So we jumped on and hid in the bathroom until the train left the station, then found a seat and waited. When the ticket guy arrived we were honest and bold.

"Sir," Erika said. "We do not have tickets, and we have no money to buy them."

He was shocked and didn't know what to do. Stop the train? Arrest us in Prague? The ball was in his court. He scoffed and walked away.

—*m*—

Back in Prague, we felt the immense relief that comes from a night promising no new hassles. Erika just wanted a hot bath to soothe her piercing. I just wanted to chill. But as I threw my coat over a chair I saw the note on the table.

> Dearest Professor Kane and the lovely Erika,
>   We discovered we have crabs. We washed your sheets and cleaned up the best we could after our treatment.
>   Sorry,
>
>   Paxus and Clara

I was annoyed. Erika was horrified. We walked out on the freezing balcony, the one overlooking the train yard's dirty brown coal cars. I remembered, then, that this was our first vacation together, something never to be forgotten. I took her hand.

"I had a great time," I said.

"Me too," she said. And she gave me that smile, the one only someone who loves someone forever gives. The one that creates an equal response that creates an equal response that creates marriage and a cancer scare and little babies and family road trips and an empty nest and elderly hands held at a dying moment. That smile.

The Silver Lining

Go Rimbaud, go Rimbaud.
And go, Johnny go, and do the watusi, oh, do the
    watusi.

Patti Smith, "Land"

Things were very dark for me for a while after the Spiral
    Tribe rave. Without meds, the voices came on like
a chorus. I was manic and out of control. I did a lot of drugs. I
wandered the streets drunk or passed my time daydreaming with
freaks. These things were true. All true.

And then there was the dreaded conversation. Exhausted upon
her return from England, Erika just stared at the wrecked flat and
at me, and I let her take a few minutes to let it all sink in. By the
following morning, she would have nowhere to live. Naturally,
she had a few questions. Extremely complex questions like, "Chuck,
what happened?" Rather than discuss it in the sour atmosphere of
the flat we'd soon be leaving, we headed to the Kamik, this amazing
boat on the Vlatava River that doubled as a bar, and over drinks I
told her everything about my mental illness and the coming-out
party. Speaking of it was something I had hoped to avoid entirely,
and not only with Erika. I didn't want anyone to know. I didn't
want the voices to define me, or at least I didn't want them to
define the way others viewed me. But I told her. She held my
hand as I got it out of my system, and when I was done, she said
something simple, something like, "Well, that explains a lot."
And that was that.

And there it was again. The silver lining.

We were holding hands on a boat, it was springtime in Prague, and Erika and I were truly falling in love.

Losing our flat was bad, but it also gave us an opportunity to test our relationship. The previous convenience of living in the same apartment had cast a doubt on our presumed love. Were we having sex just because of proximity? Would we really choose to spend our time together if we didn't share the same roof? There was only one way to find out. Erika found a new apartment, I returned to my former squat, and we started actually dating.

Thus began a good, old-fashioned courtship. There was opera, handholding along the river, drinks, dinner, coffee, picnics. I would write her over-the-top poetry, knock on her window, leave it on the sill, and run away. She would read passages of Czech novels to me. Our lives were becoming a collection of romantic postcards sold at kiosks at the end of the Charles Bridge. Idyllic and pure. Young and in love.

We became friends and then lovers again.

Later that summer, we decided the time had come to move back in together. We found another flat, this time in Pankrác, a neighborhood south of the city center. It was nothing special, but it was next to a lovely park and offered an adequate supply of hot water and two entire rooms: enough luxury, in other words, to reclaim at least some of what we'd left behind at Joy's.

But it was not utopia. Despite our newfound bliss, the neighborhood exuded a quiet hostility. The lady at the grocery store gave us mean looks and the silent treatment. Our landlady would walk into our flat without knocking and randomly yell at us. But mostly, people ignored us, so much so that we felt invisible. It was all very upsetting. We both spoke conversational Czech, so it wasn't that. But then a Czech friend reminded us that recent history might be playing a role. Many of our neighbors were older, mostly in their sixties. "Consider their lives," she reminded us. Hitler invaded Prague in 1938. He left in 1945, but then in came Stalin. And his boys didn't leave until a few years before we got there. That's fifty-odd years of some serious bullshit.

That shut us up. But we didn't quit. Instead, we thought like grandmas. When my grandmother wanted to thank, cajole, or apologize to someone, she baked for them. Baking celebrates birthdays and mends broken hearts. So Erika and I decided to make the quintessential American baked good for our neighbors: chocolate chip cookies. Unfortunately, we soon learned that Czech grocery stores didn't carry vanilla, chocolate chips, or baking powder. Even more shocking, a lot of people we'd met hadn't even heard of chocolate chip cookies. The sound of my grandmother turning over in her grave was a clarion call to action. Cookies for Pankrác!

A few weeks later, the care package from Erika's mother arrived: vanilla extract, baking powder, and a fat bag of Nestlé Toll House semi-sweet chocolate chips.

We baked for hours. The smell filled our apartment complex. Then, by the dozen and with the help of our best-rehearsed Czech, we distributed freshly baked cookies throughout our building. The folks in our apartment complex, the grocery store ladies, and even our landlady each got a plateful. In return, we earned a lot of smiles and even a few conversations. It was a shining moment of international diplomacy.

A man can't just take a lot of drugs, drink a lot, and fall in love; he also has to eat, and because eating typically requires money, it inevitably requires him to get a job. That was how I viewed work in my early years in Prague—nothing but a means to an end.

Before I met Erika, before I had neighbors to make cookies for, I spent time floundering as what can only be described as an alternative lifestyle factotum. After unsuccessfully fund-raising for the Walk across Europe, I ended up as the "marketing director" for the Tam Tam Klub, which really meant my stoned ass made a lot of elaborate cut-and-paste concert posters that the owners thought were the bee's knees. "Very Western!" they would exclaim.

Around this time, I also turned to what I liked to call "my grift." You can call it "the bullshit arts" if you like. At first I didn't really do it on purpose; it just came naturally, especially with my mania unchecked. In an Irish pub or some other English-speaking establishment, I would find an opening in the conversation and launch into one of my personal stories, which I would liberally salt with embellishments, obscenities, and self-deprecation. Inevitably someone would buy me a drink. I would milk the story for more drinks from the growing crowd. Drinks would turn into a meal and more drinks. I took the same approach toward making money. If I heard someone in a coffee shop talk about a grant they were writing, I'd interject with a few stories from my days with EYFA or the Peace Circus, and within minutes I was their editor. A magazine start-up? Consultant! I was a liaison, an advisor, a public speaker. Charm plus earnestness, topped with a touch of vaudeville panache and a smattering of desperation, made for a lethal combination.

In the midst of my grifting I got a job that lasted about a year as codirector of the Prague Social Cultural Center, located inside a decaying but airy loft building that housed a few art studios, a rehearsal space for bands, and offices for the disparate members of Prague's radical underground. I spent many nights there in my office, sleeping on tabletops to avoid the rats, a baseball bat by my side in case they got too close.

For $150 a month I ran meetings, shoveled cement, gave advice, and tried my damnedest to get my fellow codirector, a dread-locked Czech and militant PETA activist named Tomas, to stop sabotaging the center with his megalomaniacal behavior. It was a Sisyphean task, and damned if I was going to push a boulder uphill every day. I wasn't happy.

I continued to meet some great and interesting people though, and those encounters, however brief, pulled me through. I remember one American expat, a young female painter and printmaker from Manhattan who was using one of the Social Cultural Center's studios. One dreary winter's evening, when my weariness was so heavy that I laid my head on my desk just to lighten the load, she poked her head into my office and said, "You're coming with me." We walked to her studio flat, where she put on some chill jazz and drew me a bubble bath. While I sat in the tub, I enjoyed a cup of jasmine tea and her view of the city. She washed my nasty clothes and prepared a simple but elegant meal for me when I was done bathing. After dinner, we talked a bit before I fell asleep on her couch. I awoke in the morning with a blanket tucked around me and a note inviting me to enjoy some coffee and to lock the door when I left. We didn't really know each other. But her kindness was restorative, at least temporarily.

Moments like these—little reminders of the grace of humanity—are vastly underestimated, if you ask me. These little moments, ones that I'd had with the nuns in Oakland, the nurse in Haiti, and the couple in Georgia who forgave me, proclaim to us all that we are good. By simply caring for and trusting me, this woman drew the negative energy out of me like a poison.

Often, during late nights fueled by too many drugs, one of these moments would help me to pull back—to not do another line, to not put the needle in my arm, to not give up. I also think moments like these prepared me for falling in love. Because love only works when you are vulnerable. And you are vulnerable when you believe humanity is good. This was not a cool thing for a Generation Xer to believe. But I did. And I do.

—*~~*—

Most of my little jobs and grifts, combined with Erika's part-time teaching job, didn't add up to much money, and what we had mostly went toward rent, drugs, beer, and cigarettes because, well, those were our priorities. We all lived by a common credo—in Bohemia, do as the Bohemians do. So despite our love, our apartment, our newfound chocolate chip cookie–earned amity in the hood, Erika and I were basically broke.

On most days, our only honest meal was at the Hare Krishnas' restaurant. Erika and I (and a horde of others) were vegetarians at the time; Eastern Europe in the 1990s wasn't a good place for us. Our meal options were typically deep-fried cheese, deep-fried cauliflower, French fries, or a plain dumpling doused in sauerkraut. And most of that was cooked in lard. Since the Krishnas' food was both low cost and vegetarian, it was perfect. We had strong black Turkish coffee and buttered bread each morning for breakfast, and then we'd head to the Krishnas' around 3 p.m.

And along the way we traveled Prague by tram. The beauty of the city never failed to work its magic on us. For hours or even days at a time, Erika and I would sojourn in an insulated new world, population: two. We built bonfires atop Petrin Hill. Watched Gypsies pickpocket tourists on the #22. Skimmed our hands in the Vltava River on long boat rides. Hiked in the Tatra Mountains. We spent hours in the alchemy museum at Staromestske Namesti and went shopping in the street markets. We climbed water towers and danced until dawn.

--*m*--

It was during this time of wild idealism that I fulfilled a dream. I was invited to a dinner party by my friend Nic, a member of a Czech/British band called the Ecstasy of St. Teresa, whose music I adored. I arrived late, three sheets to the wind on God knows what drug. In the dining room, about fifteen people were sitting around this massive wooden table decorated in a Bohemian's dream of excess and artistic beauty. Members of my favorite band were scattered around it, as were a number of close and interesting friends. But I barely registered any of that. It was a woman I noticed. And after a few seconds of staring at each other we simultaneously remembered. Dance floor. Roxy. My first day in Prague.

Her name was Iveta, and she was a model. She was Czech, of course, and currently she had no carpeting in her hair but was completely bald. She wore a super tight Formula One racing outfit and high heels. She was intense as hell.

We kept talking, faster and faster, until—and I have no idea how this happened—we ended up in the bathroom, lights off, handcuffed together to the toilet. In the dark, I distinctly remember playing the zipper on her outfit like an instrument while she sang. Whatever you might call what we were doing was suddenly interrupted by an equally intense and fucked-up Puerto Rican jazz musician.

"Havel's at Lucerna. Right now! Let's go shake his hand."

I didn't really want to stop what I was doing—my zipper music skills were surprisingly first-rate. But I saw the Prague magic flicker in his eyes while he waited for my reply. All I could think was damn, I *would* like to shake Václav Havel's hand.

So I extricated myself from the toilet and maneuvered my way to the car of this intense and fucked-up Puerto Rican jazz musician. By the time we got to Lucerna, President Havel had just left. But the guy at the door told us where he thought Havel was headed next. It was now a quest, and our focus was epic. To shake the hand of the man who, nonviolently, brought down the Soviet Union. To shake the hand of the martyr who suffered in prison, writing some of the most amazing plays I have ever read, the poet king revered by everyone and whose list of friends included Frank Zappa and Nelson Mandela. Yes, his hand I must shake.

We went from restaurant to nightclub to restaurant, just missing him a few times. Then we saw it—a line of limousines with a security detail, stopped in front of a swanky Euro nightclub. We pulled the car up as close as we could to the limos and planned our next step. As we exited the car, however, Havel himself stepped out of the club and we were right in his path. This was too much for my intense and fucked-up Puerto Rican jazz musician friend, who quite awkwardly froze in his tracks, but not for me. Havel was my hero, goddammit! So I boldly walked up to him and, slaughtering his language, said, "Pane vy je hrdina. Děkuju" (which roughly translates as "Sir, you is hero. Thanks.") and put out my hand. He shook it and said, in perfect English, "We are all heroes." Damn.

Years later I got to speak with President Havel once again. But this time I was working as a producer for a national show on public radio. I had read that he was retiring, and I knew I had to have him on my program. I spent hours and hours sweating over what questions to ask him. When the time came, as the engineers were futzing with microphones, I considered how to break the ice before the interview officially began. Should I speak in Czech? Should I tell him we met once before? Should I even mention I lived in his country for five years? Instead I just told him, in English, that it was my great honor to have him as a guest on my program. He replied, "The honor is mine."

We are all heroes. The honor is mine. Words to live by.

Eureka: Nothing Closer
to a Man Than a Razor Blade,
Novella 2
in Homage to the Mrs.

You say my eyes
Are crazy eyes.
Sometimes they are,
And so are you.
And if you wonder
What I would do,
I would do
Anything.
If I could
You know I would.

> Jane's Addiction,
> "I Would for You"

It was one of those days when I was bouncing off the walls
and extremely manic. I wandered the streets and
ended up, as I often did, in my favorite bar, the Chapeau Rogue.
Drinking shots and getting high, however, didn't help. I could
feel a severe mania setting in.

It's worth noting here that none of us had phones—there were
certainly no cell phones yet, but no one had landlines in their
flats, either. So if you wanted to hang out with your mates, you

would simply drift between your common meet-up spots. It was inefficient, but it was kind of fun and spontaneous, too. I began looking for Erika the moment I stepped into the Chapeau Rogue. I thought maybe we could hang out at home alone and talk or something. But she wasn't around. I knew I was headed for mischief if I didn't find something to occupy myself, so I went to look for her at our flat back in Pankrác.

As I paced the tram on my ride home, I thought of our bathroom, a cozy space decked out with pink tiles and centered around a large sunken tub. *I am going to have a bath in that tub. That will relax me. A nice hot bath would be just the trick.* I gave a few scratches to my five-day-old scruffy beard. *A bath and a shave. Perfect.*

I stopped at the store on the way home and got a twenty-four-pack of disposable razors and some shaving cream.

I entered my flat, a rolling wave of mania still unsettling my belly, though I was optimistic about my plan. I rolled a fat joint and smoked it in my hot bath. I then grabbed the mirror, applied the shaving cream to my face, and started to shave. I found that the process was unbelievably calming. I liked the focus required to shave the bits on my upper lip, below my chin, next to my ear. When I finished, I felt the mania well up again. So I smoked another joint and shaved my head. The clean look of no beard or hair was mesmerizing to me. But more was needed.

More lather, a new blade, and off went my eyebrows and even my eyelashes. I hadn't felt more relaxed in ages, although I did gash my left eyebrow pretty bad, enough to turn my bath water a light shade of pink. I smoked another joint. I shaved my armpits and chest—slicing a nipple while I was at it.

I drained the now cold tub, wiped away the hair with an old T-shirt, then refilled it and got back to work. I'd smoked far too much weed by now, throwing off my equilibrium and making me more than a little careless. I went to work on my legs and even the hair on my toes. Pretty soon I was cut to hell and bleeding like mad. I was also running through my disposable razors too fast. I knew I'd need a few sharp ones for my genitals (those I was saving for last). I was so high and so into this process at this point that I just went for it—dull disposables or not. With a mantra of "don't cut your balls dude" running through my mind I survived with my cock and balls uncut.

The rest of me, however, was a mess. I exited the tub and stood in front of the full-length mirror of my pink bathroom. I couldn't stop staring at my hairless body with little rivulets of blood running down it. I felt alive and very zen. And I wanted to share this sense of peace immediately with Erika, my true love. So I covered my body with the only thing I could find to staunch the bleeding—baby powder. I was now a very-stoned Casper the Friendly Ghost with coagulated lines of blood all over him. Which I found to be very impressive.

I excitedly put on my combat boots and leather trench coat and nothing else as I headed for the door, intent on returning to the Chapeau Rogue to find Erika. Luckily for me, and for Erika, she was at the door as I opened it to leave. I mistook her shocked silence for an empathy of sorts, as though she was awed by my brave attempt at self-expression. I slowly dropped the trench coat to the floor and smiled, allowing her to take in my newly majestic body. What I got in return was a little head tilt of disappointment and an exasperated sigh. What she said next I had heard many times before and would hear many times after. But hearing these words at that exact moment brought tears of joy to my eyes.

"Jesus Christ, Chuck, you're such an idiot." But she didn't leave. She lit a cigarette and went into the bedroom to get a grip. When she came out she gave me a good long look over, and took me out to our local for some beers. What a woman.

Open for Suggestions

Well, ain't got no spare, you ain't got no jack,
You don't give a shit you ain't never coming back.
Maybe you're standing on the corner of 17th and
    Wazee Streets.
Out in front of the Terminal Bar,
There's a Thunderbird moon in a Muscatel sky.
You've been drinking cleaning products all night,
Open for suggestions.

Tom Waits, "Nighthawk Postcards"

Eventually, Erika and I grew tired of poverty, and because we were young, educated Americans with at least a few job skills in our pockets, we decided it was time to get real jobs for a while.

Erika took a job running a vegetarian restaurant above a nightclub called the Radost FX. This was *the* club in Prague, the place where Euro Club MTV set up live broadcasts, where actors and models went to be noticed. I took a much different job at the Sports Bar Praha as a fry cook. It paid a lot, the work was easy, and, most importantly, I didn't have to think. It was a place where Americans (and Czechs who wanted to marry them) hung out to get a burger and fries and watch *Seinfeld* or *The Simpsons*. Sure, making chicken fingers for American embassy workers wasn't my idea of paradise, but I needed a break from everything. I was ready and willing for the next idea—I just needed a breather first. And to have enough money to buy soap.

It was during this time that Erika's fashion sense started to have an effect on me. The fact that Erika not only shaved her legs and her underarms but also wore makeup was something of a revelation. All my old hippie girlfriends wore patchouli and bangles. Erika wore perfume and dresses—and not patchwork quilt dresses or batik ones, either. I remember one day she went out wearing a red dress with matching enameled chopsticks piercing the bun in her hair. She was plucking her eyebrows and looking fine. I looked at my worn out Guatemala pants and ripped T-shirt and sorry excuse for a beard and knew it was time for a change. I headed to the secondhand stores and bought several old Czech grandpa suits. I wore them loose over tight-collared white shirts I left untucked. For my feet, I purchased combat boots, which I shined, and I shaved my head to the scalp and sculpted a pristine goatee. I was no Erika, but this was all such a massive departure that I felt like a fashion model.

Fashion was not foremost on the minds of the clientele at Sports Bar Praha, who were mostly boring Americans in khakis. There were some exceptions, however. One regular was a Brit named Mark.

When I met him, Mark was recovering from a coma and pancreas-removal surgery, stemming from a regretful night of binge drinking absinthe. He was tall, skinny, and always dressed in black—a uniform comprising concert T-shirts, leather pants, and a rubber trench coat. In his earlobe he wore a human finger bone he'd stolen from a Czech grave years earlier. He was the antithesis of my past—he was a cynical intellectual with little or no sense of morality. He was also an artist who drew complicated and dark pointillist scenes—bleak alcoholic nightmares, skeletal and unforgiving of the human spirit. We hit it off immediately. Not because we had the same world vision but because I found him a romantic figure—right out of central casting. I was ready to meet a guy like Mark. And as it turns out, he was looking for a guy like me.

We began reading books together at his place while he convalesced. You'd be surprised how much you learn reading *The Protocols of the Elders of Zion* with a Jew of Russian heritage who wears a human finger in his ear. Over time, we developed a routine of drinking coffee in front of his fancy computer, foraging through this new thing called "the internet," which impressed us both very much. With our dial-up connection, it may have taken five minutes to load an image, but what images! And we had time to spare.

The internet—as it is wont to do—got us thinking. Mark, who had recently (and mysteriously) come into a large amount of money, was looking to invest in an idea but didn't want to do any actual work. I really wanted to work on an idea but didn't have any money. It was, in that sense, a match made in heaven. Soon, the idea for the Terminal Bar, East Europe's first internet café, was born. Goodbye short-order cook. Hello chief operating officer.

———

Also around this time, Erika and I started a relationship with our friend Adela. And by relationship I mean just how it sounds—a three-way affair. From a distance it seems odd, but at the time, it seemed perfectly normal. Erika and I were dating, we were serious, but each one of us had feelings for Adela, and vice versa. We drank together. We did drugs together. We hung out a lot. And we had a lot of great sex. So we went for it. I can remember many a night with each one of them by my side, wondering how long it would last. There were no models to duplicate or even refer to. We were charting new ground.

It didn't last more than six months. In reality, it never had a chance. Erika and I were already living together; our intimate bond was just closer than the bond she or I had with Adela. In retrospect it was never really fair to Adela. But I cared about her, about the three of us, and I know Erika did as well. When Erika and I got married in St. Louis years later, Adela flew from Prague to be in the wedding. She presented us with a beautiful homemade quilt of the Charles Bridge she'd made. I remember looking at her during the wedding and thinking that this is how love can be. And on winter nights when Erika and I put that quilt on our bed I am reminded that no one should ever tell another how to love.

Now before you start thinking, "Hey, Chuck's getting his shit together!" I should disclose one other thing. Around the time I left the sports bar, I discovered meth. And so did Erika and Adela. We did it all the time.

I'll be honest: I ♥ meth. Its initial appeal for me was that it was the prototypical "hard-core drug," a new frontier beyond the nice, hippie vibes of LSD, Ecstasy, and pot. Meth was mean. It brought the user to uncomfortable edges, and part of me liked the idea that it was so addictive. But I'll be frank. Just as someone who hears voices should not take acid, so a person with manic disorder should not use meth. Hell, I shouldn't drink coffee, let alone snort the ditch-speed, bathtub gin of hard drugs.

In Prague, meth came from the Russian mob. They called it "pico." We did it all the time, and we loved it. Erika and I and our friends would stay up forever smoking cartons of cigarettes and "spinning" (or, as my friend Antony called it, "hole drilling"), in which a subject would be discussed with such intensity and speed for hours and hours that we would start to spin in metaphorical, and at times literal, circles. We'd grit our teeth so hard that our jaws ached the next day. It was a painful pleasure, and we had a grand old time. As Erika put it, "I've learned what I can learn from acid. I just want to get fucked up."

Erika and I began regularly doing pico and were soon invited to these amazing, drugged-out private parties. They'd be held on boats floating on the Vltava River or inside a store that sold nothing but blue jeans. The parties were great, but the day after usually wasn't. The pico crash is rough, so Erika and I established an agreement—when coming down, we must be gentle. No conflict was allowed on any subject for any reason. Positive energy, baby!

Of course, not everyone shared our agreement. Sometimes, the darkness would descend.

My weed dealer was a Danish man named Pjort. I partied with him a few times but didn't really know anything about him other than he was a reliable source of good marijuana. One night—and I remember it was near the end of a wonderful summer, when acid jazz had infiltrated Prague, and more specifically my old hangout, the Roxy, with positive, danceable, and upbeat music—things got dark.

Around five in the morning, closing time, I bought hashish from Pjort in the Roxy bathroom and could see he was struggling but not ready to call it a night. Both his nostrils were bleeding from fresh lines, and he was worried about his eyes. "Can't blink man," he said. "Can't blink."

I tried to reassure him that in fact he was blinking, that his eyes would be fine. I patted him on the back and brought him some toilet paper to wipe his face.

"Take it easy," I said. "We're professionals at this, man. Ride the storm."

With that modicum of reassurance, we left him, and Erika, Adela, and I went back to our place to come down by watching VCR tapes of the *X-Files* and smoking hash and having sex. As I later learned, Pjort chose another route. He went to our Israeli friend Mishy's flat with about ten others—the truly hard-core members of our crew. Whereas we would start using on Friday and end Sunday morning, they would go until Tuesday, often mixing other drugs with the meth. Sometimes, they scared me. What happened next—as told to me a dozen different times on trams, over coffee in cafés, and over beer in the coming weeks—became legend in the Prague drug counterculture.

Inside the apartment, a young Czech woman having a rough come-down had curled up in a chair, hoping to quietly wait out the pico's effects. But Pjort was all over her. He wanted to kiss her. Everyone kept tugging at him, telling him to leave her in peace, but he kept at it until someone forcibly shoved him away. He apologized and retreated to the bathroom, and the tension in the room subsided. Minutes later, however, Pjort bolted out of the bathroom naked with a hard-on, leapt on the woman, and tried to bite her neck vampire-style.

A person on pico has superhuman strength. But Pjort wasn't the only superman in the room. The others grabbed him and threw him into the hallway naked and screaming. The neighbors, an elderly Czech couple, heard all of this and, unfortunately, the woman opened her door. Pjort turned his vengeance on her, pouncing for another bite. From inside the door, the husband quickly produced a hand ax, which he proceeded to whack on the top of Pjort's head. Blood spurted from the gash in his skull. Mishy told us later that a torrent of it ran down the cement stairs.

Pjort survived. Luckily. But if this was what could happen to a brain on meth, you might wonder why we kept at it, why we kept playing at the edges and spinning when there was plain evidence that things could go so wrong.

Enter the wedding of Antony and Marketa.

Antony was an American with a PhD from MIT in nuclear engineering. He was working as a safety engineer at a nuclear power plant—the same plant I'd tried to stop not that long before. Before we met, other expats kept telling me I should meet him. "He works at Temelin," they'd say. "He's just like you, but, like, your enemy."

Eventually, Erika and I did meet Antony and his girlfriend, Marketa, a beautiful, intense Czech woman with a shaved head and take-no-shit attitude. Despite our presumed enmity over nuclear power, we did some meth together and hit it off swimmingly. More than swimmingly, actually. For a couple years, we were inseparable on weekends. Erika and Marketa would leave Antony and I alone for hours at some club while they danced and flirted, and we would just talk together, as fast as we could. He was a hard guy from South Boston with a chip on his shoulder, and he loved taking things one step too far. And damn did he love meth. He'd start in on Friday after work and go until Sunday morning, then take the rest of the day to recover. He was always fresh as a daisy on Monday morning. It sounds unlikely that a nuclear safety engineer on meth was in control of his life. But he was.

Over a Sunday meal at the home of Marketa's mother, who also lived in Pankrác, the happy couple announced their news— they were getting married. After the celebratory champagne, the details emerged. They had rented a castle in a small Bohemian town. The castle could sleep one hundred. The ceremony would have a medieval theme, with horses and music, jousting and sword fighting. There would be period costumes for all. Carriages. A suckling pig on a spit. There would also be meth and Ecstasy galore. And one more thing: the priest for the ceremony would be yours truly.

Recently, Erika and I pulled out the photos from the wedding. There's Erika in her white face makeup and heavy black eyeliner, wearing a black hooded robe. There I was in a gold and white bishop's uniform from the 1800s, miter and all. We remembered the jousts, the goblets, the drugs, the over-the-topness of every damn detail. The photos revealed more than details, though. We remembered the sincerity of the ceremony I created for them. Antony and Marketa were so in love, and everyone was so happy for them and for the collective we. We were happy to be alive in a time when these were the choices we made.

So, yes, we did meth. But we did it well, and we did it with full enthusiasm.

———

Again, if I were to revisit this younger version of myself now, I would give him some advice, but this time it would be more concrete. Do not open a business in Eastern Europe, especially only years after the fall of the Soviet Union. Especially if you don't know squat about running a business and if your rubber-suit-wearing business partner awakens at 3 p.m. every day. If you do these things, your life will, I'm afraid, be very difficult.

But damn if I wasn't determined to make the Terminal Bar work anyway. Because at this point in my life I had figured something out. I like to work. I like projects. I am a producer at heart, in that I like to foster and shepherd creative ideas through to completion. I was completely ready to sink my teeth deep into something. To really spend some years making a project happen. And this was just that sort of project—over my head, complicated, requiring heaps of idealism, and I was in charge of it.

Launching our dream required us to weave our way through Kafkaesque bureaucratic labyrinths. Our method was simple: throw money at everyone. Using Mark's cash, we bribed officials and paid off construction bosses. Renting was such a nightmare that we bought an entire building in downtown Prague. We hired Borek Sipek—the man who designed the furniture for Havel's Prague Castle office—to design our kiosks and bar stools. We even knocked out one room's floor and erected a bridge inside— which we gilded. In gold. And then we built an internet backbone (a T-1 line, unheard of in Eastern Europe at the time) in a country where most people didn't have a phone.

As the money flowed, our dream grew. In addition to an internet café we wanted a top-notch espresso bar and full alcohol bar. We wanted an esoteric bookstore, an avant-garde cinema. Since we had one of the most powerful internet infrastructures in the country we decided to launch a web design company as well. And while we were at it, hell, we thought we might start an internet service provider company, the biggest and fastest one in the Czech Republic.

All these ideas needed people to run them. They needed budgets and office space and structure and meetings and inspiration. And that's where I, the chief operating officer, came in. I quickly took to the role of the inspirational, Mr. Pep Talk manager. And it wasn't just for the staff, which in a few months' time numbered nearly thirty. The entire expat community in Prague was sold. Sure, I was a mess in a million ways, but so were they. Yet I know when something magical is happening, and this was it.

But the magic would take time. And lots of patience. One of the ways we sustained the dream—both for ourselves and our supporters—was by hosting something we called "shock nights." At the Roxy, we set up a film projector and screened what we considered shocking Western movies, which we followed with talks by guest lecturers. We hired people to write subtitles for the movies and to translate the lectures into both Czech and English. For example, we showed the Japanese cyberpunk fantasy film *Tetsuo: The Iron Man* and had a lecture afterward on transhumanism. To our surprise, about 250 people showed up. We were quite pleased with ourselves.

But we were stunned when, at our seventh showing, about a thousand folks came to see *Clockwork Orange*, a film that apparently struck a chord for the mostly young Czech folks in the audience. Its content would have been enough to rattle any East European at the time. But it was the after-movie lecture that put the evening over the top. We invited the leader of the Czech fascist party to speak—a questionable decision at best. He showed up with a dozen or so "security" detail with shaved heads wearing suspenders and jackboots. They cheered during the beating scenes, and during the infamous rape scene they stood and Heil Hitlered the screen. The crowd was on edge. I remember standing in the balcony next to the sound guy and Erika as the lecture started. A few scuffles ensued, and at one point it seemed a riot was imminent. But cooler heads prevailed. And after it was done, we felt we'd scored a point for free speech that day and another for the legend of the Terminal Bar.

We knew we were on to something when *Newsweek* ran an article about us, trumpeting the pending opening of the first internet café in Eastern Europe.

After almost two years of planning, renovating, interior designing, and endless permit seeking, a process complicated by money problems, the internet café part of our dream was about to happen. Our investment—well, Mark's investment—now eclipsed $900,000. The staff had been working full time for almost eighteen months and the Terminal Bar at Soukenická 6, Prague 1, was about to be the countercultural sensation of the decade.

And I was at the center of it all. I felt alive again.

Eureka: A Hail Mary Toss, Novella 3 in Homage to the Mrs.

Not by pennies dimes nor quarters,
But with happy sons and daughters,
And they'll sing around Stromboli,
Ingrid Bergman.

Woody Guthrie, "Ingrid Bergman"

When war broke out in former Yugoslavia in 1992, many young Serbs fled to Prague to avoid forced conscription and, like many of us, live a more Bohemian life. Erika was still a manager at the Radost FX, and soon she had several Serbian co-workers. She got to know two of them well— Natasha and Dejan. Like us, they were young and in love. They wanted to get married, but it was impossible for Dejan to go back home since he was viewed as an army deserter. But their love persisted, and eventually the war, like all wars, came to an end. They announced that they would get married in the summer of 1997, in their home town of Arandelovac. We, of course, were honored to be invited to attend.

At the time Arandelovac was not accessible by train from Prague. We got a ride for the nine-hour drive from Katka, a woman Erika knew, who dated Darko, Dejan's brother. The hot trip in a chugging Czech-made Skoda would have been bad enough without sharing the backseat with a wiggly, very pregnant dog that smelled like hell and specialized in vaginal discharges.

"She is due any day," Katka said, patting the dog's distended belly, "and I didn't want to leave her alone."

I just rolled down the window and smoked a lot of cigarettes.

In Arandelovac, we were put up in the best hotel in town—the Hotel Star Zdanje. Unfortunately, the war had not spared even the best hotel in town. Basic maintenance had been ignored and its very foundations were crumbling. More notably, most of the rooms had been converted into a recovery hospital for injured soldiers. Men with no legs and bandaged heads roamed the grounds with tired nurses by their sides. Our room came free of charge with a decomposing animal on the floor. Still, the protocol of the gracious foreign guest was maintained. We cleared out the carcass and made the best of our circumstances.

⁓

The Serbian Orthodox wedding was a full-on, three-day affair. For many this was the first real party since the war ended. They did it right with feasts and dancing and singing and drinking. And even more drinking. At the time I spoke decent Czech, which was similar to Serbian, so I was able to communicate just enough to understand my role at this wedding. The job of the men was to get everyone drunk. I was handed a bottle of homemade slivovitz (plum skin brandy, my favorite alcohol in the world) and was instructed to give shots to the guests and bring it back empty by the end of the day. I did my job. This was repeated for three days.

There were many other customs, all foreign to me, happening left and right. But it was all beautiful and interesting, and it felt like a great honor to be there.

On the second day, after the groom's father ritually bought the bride from her father, there was a great feast and party at the house of the groom's family. Scores of picnic tables lined the yard and road in front of the house. Accordions played, singers sang, much pork was passed, and slivovitz flowed.

Other than Czechs, Erika and I were the only foreigners there. We tried to explain that we had driven only nine hours to get to the wedding from Prague, but a rumor was started that we had traveled all the way from America for Dejan and Natasha. Many of their family members were greatly honored that we came. That explains why a group of men grabbed me and insisted I sit at a table with them. These were former soldiers, some still in uniforms, who ranged from ages eighteen to fifty, and they all claimed to be cousins of Natasha, which I can't imagine is possible, but then again, maybe I was misunderstanding their Serbian in my slivovitz and pork haze. When I sat down, the remaining women at the table, in unison, got up and left. A special bottle of slivovitz appeared with a corn cob stopper, along with a dirty glass. It was time to get down to drinking.

But what appeared next really got my attention. A gun was placed next to the bottle and the glass. All three items were presented to me—the honored guest. I'd noticed that folks had been shooting guns at different times during this wedding; they may not have had access to fireworks, but with a war just over everyone had firearms and ammo. I had never shot a gun before and was, preposterously, more afraid of making an ass out of myself in front of these men than killing someone. So I did what I had to do. I poured a deep glass and pounded it. As I exhaled a fiery breath, I grabbed the gun, closed my eyes, put it above my head, flinched, and shot. This was a crowd pleaser, and for the rest of the wedding, every time I saw one of Dejan's or Natasha's male relatives, they would put a finger gun above their head, say "pow!" and laugh at my not-very-manly shooting.

———

On the third and final day, the wedding ceremony itself took place. It was held in a sixteenth-century Serbian Orthodox church trimmed in gold leaf and lined with gorgeous oil paintings of saints. The ceremony was beautiful, but I understood none of it. After it was over, Natasha stood on the steps of the church with all the single women lined up behind her. This, I realized, was something I could wrap my head around: she was going to throw the bouquet. I saw Erika in the crowd. Her multicolored hair contrasted beautifully with the black flower print on her low-cut tan dress. As Natasha launched the bouquet over her head, I watched it curve through the air like a game-saving Hail Mary toss right into Erika's arms.

The party after the wedding was hosted by the groom's father. I remember little of it. I am sure there was more singing and dancing and pork and slivovitz.

Erika and I danced for hours, and as the party started to wind down we made our way back to Hotel Star Zdanje. As we walked through Arandelovac I glanced at her just as she was smelling the bouquet. That was that. I got on one knee (unsteadily, perhaps) and asked her to marry me. I wished for a gun to shoot in the air, to make a noise for all who could hear when this woman, this woman of my dreams, said yes. But a kiss would do.

The Italians

Standing on the shoulders of giants leaves me cold.
A mean idea to call my own, a hundred million
  birds fly away.

Everybody hit the ground, everybody hit the
  ground.

REM, "King of Birds"

Leaving my fiancée Erika and our lover Adela snuggling
naked in bed, I grabbed my bong and sucked down
an enormous, satisfying toke in the kitchen. The sun was just rising
outside, and I was struggling to suppress the voices that were likewise rising. "Give me a fucking break, man. I'm on to something
here. Just leave me alone for a while." I had spent more than four
years in Prague and almost three years off my meds. There were
ups and there were downs. I could always feel the downs coming,
but usually when the voices kicked in, I just took off, literally or
with drugs, and let others attribute my wanderings to an eccentric
personality. But I didn't want to take off anymore. Certainly not
now. I had work to do and I was excited to get going.

Opening day for the Terminal Bar was just weeks away. Sure,
we still didn't have glass in the windows or even tables, but hell,
Newsweek had written about us. I gave myself a hard look in the
mirror, psyched myself up with a little speech, and pretended like
I wasn't scared I might go completely insane. The rest of the fear I
masked with weed. I pulled on some pants and rubbed the sleep
from my eyes, which were rimmed with dark circles but alive with

the possibilities of the day. I buttoned my shirt as I paced in and out of the bedroom muttering "time to make the donuts" until the girls told me to beat it.

My job that day was to organize our grand opening. I had big dreams. Jello Biafra of the Dead Kennedys would pump up the crowd with some spoken word, then Lydia Lunch would hit them with "Atomic Bongos" before Noam Chomsky laid out some heavy shit about how our business was the kind of panacea our material world needed. I wanted a ribbon cutting, live music, all of it.

I hopped on the #18 tram into the city center, eating a poppy seed *kolac* as I watched the sunrise bounce off the red rooftops and spires of the city's skyline. In my shitty concrete block of an apartment, I often forgot that Prague wasn't just a former Soviet state. This very old city—which largely avoided the bombs of both world wars—was also a stunning place where kings once employed alchemists. That ridiculous quest to turn lead into gold was a form of idealism that I felt flowing through me today. Back in my bed, I had two women. In front of me was yet another day of making something from nothing—a new business I'd helped create that would soon be a glittering addition to this incredible city. As the train rumbled along, the sugar and pot in my system were crashing happily into a growing sense of gratitude and awe.

I got off the tram at Staroměstské Náměstí alongside the Vltava River and walked up Revoluční to Soukenická where the Terminal Bar was. The walk was unnecessary; I could have taken the red line underground directly from our house at Pankrác. But why travel underneath Prague when I could take in its wonders at ground level? I bought a pack of cigarettes at a kiosk. Today, the shopkeepers, the folks headed to work or making deliveries, seemed less romantic than they usually did to me when I would see them as I was on my way home from a night out, still drunk or coming off drugs, less like objects, and more human. They reminded me not of the Bohemians I called friends but of my working-class roots. People who actually worked for a living—in car factories and in steel mills. It was just one more reminder of how sick and tired I was of being a pseudo-grifter, of bullshitting and sweet-talking in order to get my next meal. And now I had the opportunity to roll up my sleeves and do some real work. *I need to get up early more often*, I remember thinking.

I arrived at the Terminal Bar. And there, my heart that had been full and rising fell once again off the cliff.

Something was very, very wrong. The windows and front doors were covered in plywood, the lights were off inside. I stupidly fumbled in my pocket for my keys, then realized they wouldn't work on the new padlock and chain that locked the front doors. Searching for clues, I spotted two men in double-breasted suits sitting in a small Czech car parked across the narrow street. Sensing trouble, I hightailed it to Mark's apartment.

When a guy who usually sleeps in until three o'clock in the afternoon answers the first ring at half past dawn, you know something's up. Mark looked like he'd been crying. He fingered the bone in his ear, and over his shoulder I noticed, sitting alone on the kitchen table, a shoebox.

He waves me in and we walk to it.

"Open it up," he says.

Inside was the eye of a cow.

I don't know if you've seen a cow eye that has been pulled out of its socket before, but it's surprisingly big. And bloody. Veins and grey gelatinous strands of ick had formed a dark stain beneath it. I remember my first thought. *How the hell did they get it out of the skull? A jig saw? Their bare hands?* Then my attention went to the sentence, written in English and apparently with blood, on the inside cover of the box: "Pay up, bitch."

Praying that this is just some elaborate practical joke, I say, "What the fuck is this?"

"Chuck, you need to sit down. We need to talk."

And just like that, I knew what was coming. I knew everything I was about to hear was going to be a big steaming pile of bullshit. And I knew that pile was about to cover, stink up, and make a mockery of not only that morning's wellspring of hope and optimism but the past few years of my life. Maybe my entire life. Bullshit, bullshit, bullshit. Jesus was bullshit. College was bullshit. Being an activist was bullshit. I'd been scamming people to make money, inspiring them as their leader to some greater good, faking my way to twenty-nine years old. I'd been banking on Mark and his money and the possibilities of the internet to magically morph into something real and exciting because my other prospects were otherwise nonexistent. What was I going to do? Work in a bar my whole life? Teach English? I didn't even have money for a plane ticket home (wherever that was). I was, remarkably, in the exact same predicament as when I arrived in Prague years earlier. Dammit.

"Chuck, I didn't inherit any money."

I held his gaze for a long moment, then dropped my head and let out a long, pent-up breath.

"Yeah, no shit."

All the suspicions I'd harbored during my time working with Mark came in a flash. This guy—a cynic, an artist, a spewer of esoterica, an intellectual who struggled to eat more than a hard-boiled egg each day and lived off café crèmes and Camels—he was going to start a multimillion-dollar business? This pancreas-missing alcoholic was my savior? Sure, Chuck. Keep on believing.

I didn't sit down. Instead, we stood there in his swanky loft apartment with its twenty-five-foot ceilings and arched windows offering stunning views of Old Town Square, the apartment Mark shared with his beautiful model-of-a-girlfriend, Katka. The walls were hung with art, and the air was tinged with the smell of plush leather couches warming in the sun. For Christmas one year, Erika and I had joined them here for a turkey meal with all the trimmings. But now there was a cow's eye in a box and some story behind it.

So Mark starts explaining some things, starting with his girlfriend.

The beautiful Katka grew up in Verona, he told me, because her father was a government worker, a diplomat, under Communism. That's why she speaks Italian.

"Okay?" I said.

She made some good friends back in high school, Mark explains. Now she's doing some business with them. With these Italian guys.

Things were becoming more clear. "Mobsters," I said.

Now pacing, Mark spit out more of the story, in which the Chechen mob also figured. I mentally filled in enough details to realize we'd been caught up in a classic shell game. At a time when formerly state-owned property was rapidly being privatized, the Chechens had poured money into the post-Communist vacuum and now had a stronghold within the Prague housing and black markets. Meanwhile, Katka, with her Italian connections, had access to "real money" that the Chechens liked. Czech currency wasn't even real yet, but an American dollar, a deutsche mark, an Italian lire—those had meaning in the black market. With her dual citizenship, Katka also filled the role of "owner" of our budding establishment because only Czechs could own land. In short, our building had been purchased from the Chechens and was now accruing big-time equity for the Italians. Everyone was making money and could have been quite happy. But there was one problem: Katka had been skimming off the top. Skimming off the top between the Chechen and Italian mobs. I'll give her this: the girl had balls.

"She needed to clean that skimmed money without using the black market," Mark said.

"You mean she needed someone who didn't know what he or she was doing to run a business for her," I said.

I laid out what I suspected Mark's role was. Katka needed someone who wouldn't stay within a budget, who was loose with bookkeeping, who would take too long to finish what he started, and in the process act as an unwilling money launderer.

Mark was silent. I looked at the cow eye and felt a little wave of nausea.

Katka's scheme, and her pico habit, had gotten out of control, Mark mumbled. Too much money went missing, and the Chechens noticed.

"I can't expect you to believe this," he said, "but I've bought into the idea of Terminal Bar. I want it to open. I want it to happen. I believe in it now."

More truth or more bullshit?

"But right now," he continued, "if the Chechens don't get $125,000 in the next seventy-two hours, they're going to kill her."

Then Mark, my friend who had obviously lied repeatedly to me, the guy with whom I had often played video games until dawn, the guy whose art I admired, who had introduced me to Radiohead and taught me how to view life differently than I ever had before, looked up at me with a new emotion in his usually cynical eyes. He was scared.

There was some good news, he said. Katka was still making the Italians a lot of money. They knew her. They were willing to forgive. And in Italy, they had the cash—$125,000 to pay off the Chechen mob and $125,000 to fix Katka's "mess," a certain building that was earmarked to be the first internet café in Eastern Europe—to keep the whole mess flowing.

<hr />

It was Erika who, a year earlier, got me interested in opera. One stunningly perfect spring evening she convinced me to see *Rigoletto* at the Statni Opera in Prague. Sung in Italian with the libretto in Czech, the plot and words flew past me, but I admired its grandiosity, its flair for over-the-top tragedy. During the entire performance, a young girl in a white dress at stage right rocked slowly on an oversized rocking horse. At the show's climax, poor Rigoletto, thirsty for revenge against the prince who had raped his daughter, unwittingly stabs and kills his only daughter, who is hidden inside a burlap bag. As the sword plunged, the little girl at stage right stopped rocking. That was enough for me: I was sold.

Later that year, Erika and I decided we needed a Western vacation. After some research, we learned about the annual Verdi opera festival in Verona, where the greatest singers in the world perform in the Arena di Verona, a Roman amphitheater built in AD 30. *Perfetto!* Unfortunately, it'd be an expensive trip, and we were so very *not* rich. Mark and Katka, however, had a Verona connection: they arranged for us to stay with their friend Antonio.

I'd met Antonio once before, in Prague, a few months earlier. We'd talked opera for hours in an outdoor café near the Prague Castle, drinking Campari and espresso. I spent the whole time trying not to stare at his immaculate alligator skin shoes, his linen pants, the silk scarf tied loosely around his neck, or the sunglasses that neatly matched his belt buckle. When Mark and Katka told me Antonio would take care of us, I believed them.

For the Verdi festival, we took the train from Prague to Verona. Antonio was waiting for us at the station, looking dapper as ever. He drove us to an apartment complex far from the city. It was a strange place. Dozens of fully furnished apartments, seemingly new, were ready for occupants, yet the entire complex was empty, and few other buildings were in sight. The area was surrounded by olive groves and acres of fruit trees, all of it owned by Antonio's family. Our apartment, though beautiful, appeared to have been unoccupied for years. Layers of dust covered everything. After we set our bags down, Antonio pressed a key in my palm, then paused and held my eyes for a few beats—was he trying to convey that I now owed him something?—and said to meet him in an hour at the tratorria up the street.

After unpacking, we walked through his family's peach orchards on our way to an idealized version of a tratorria—from the tricolored awning and handmade wood tables to the straw covered chianti bottles with candles dripping down them. Hams were hanging, and a huge cheese wheel sat on a counter next to a pile of fresh fruit. Antonio invited us to a table, holding the chair out for Erika, and informed us that this place, too, was his family's. The server and cook, in fact, was his own portly mother. His cousins played guitar and lightly hit a tambourine from a nearby table while drinking grappa. Over the next two hours, we were served mountains of food, from grilled peaches wrapped in prosciutto to spicy seafood pasta to succulent pork chops and steamed artichoke hearts. Breads and cheeses and olives and different vinegars—it kept coming and coming. We talked and laughed and listened to his cousins sing.

Two days later Antonio arranged for us to see *Aida*. The performance was delightfully extravagant—at one point costumed elephants trudged across a two-tier stone stage—and it ended with the star-crossed lovers in each other's arms in a sealed cave awaiting their tragic fate—*O terra, addio*. The next day, after thanking Antonio for his hospitality, we hitchhiked to Lago de

Garde, Italy's largest lake, then made our way to Venice, where we spent four lazy days sleeping on park benches and drinking wine from our water bottles. It was, in the end, just the vacation we'd been looking for, and Antonio had made it possible.

"Chuck, I can't travel. I'm too sick."

This was Mark, pulling the old-absinthe-binge-coma-pancreas-removal excuse. Fucking classic.

"Travel where?" I asked.

"To Verona. That's where Antonio lives. You remember Antonio, right? He's Katka's Italian partner. He says he only trusts me and you."

Fuck. So Antonio was mafia. I knew his shoes were too nice for a peach farmer.

Here's what was asked of me. Over the next seventy-two hours I had to drive from Prague to Verona, about an eight-hour trip. I needed to pick up $250,000 from the Italian mafia. Then I needed to drive back, crossing the borders of Italy, Austria, Germany, and the Czech Republic (and because this was before the EU, these borders were very real). Then I needed to give the Chechen mafia $125,000 to save Katka's life and use the rest of the money to save our dream—the Terminal Bar. Seventy-two hours. And, oh yeah, I don't know how to drive. When the other kids at Chalker High School in Southington, Ohio, were taking driver's ed, I'd been saving souls in the Philippines and Haiti.

Enter Dee. A Brixton filmmaker and one of the core folks at the Terminal Bar, Dee, like me, had bought into the dream hook, line, and sinker. He was one of my best friends in the world. With Dee as my driver, we at least had a chance.

I met up with Dee at a restaurant that overlooked the Terminal Bar site. Over "hamneggs" (yes, that's how it was spelled it on the menu) I explained the situation and did my best to persuade him.

"Look, it's a buddy flick," I said. "It's a road trip movie. It's a mob caper with a ticking clock. And we get to save the day. Why not?"

It worked. "Fuck it, I'll go," he said.

Over the next few hours we packed and developed a plan as precious sand fell through the hourglass.

- A backpack to put the money in: *check*.
- Dress clothes so we don't look like the couple of losers that we were: *check*. Dee went with a bolo tie and a new suit embroidered with fifty-two playing cards. I went with a bow tie and classy green velvet suit. I looked like a putting green with a six-inch goatee. *'Sup, ladies?*
- A car to get us there: *check*. Taking Katka's seemed appropriate. Her grey Czech-made Skoda was perfectly nondescript. We didn't note the irony that *skoda* in Czech also means "pity." Or hell, maybe we did.

Before we pull away Dee takes out a coin.

"Heads or tails," he says.

"Um, heads?"

Heads it was. He pulls out some pico, and we both do a bump. And our heroes are off and away.

It was midnight or so when the lights of Verona appeared before us. Wired and tense, we navigated our way to the hotel. Mark had told us we'd stay somewhere "inconspicuous." "Just a place to spend the night," he'd said.

"Fucking hell," Dee said. "It's a four-star fucking hotel."

And we had the grand suite, of course. Apparently Mark felt he could buy his way out of his own guilt.

In our ridiculous suits as Dee's new eyebrow piercing festered, we "inconspicuously" checked in with our empty backpack under our real, preregistered names.

To calm our nerves, we'd planned on hitting the room's minibar, but of course they didn't have one because that kind of place wouldn't. Their alcohol was all room service, all top shelf.

We order cognac "and some of that shit that tastes like orange." They bring it up. We immediately slam shots. And because we wanted to keep the "buddy road-trip" vibe going, before the bell-hop left, we got him to dial a phone sex line for us. The woman we got spoke English.

"No," I told her. "We want a woman who speaks Italian."

"I don't speak Italian."

"Jesus, this is Italy. I want a woman who speaks Italian, goddammit!"

It took a few minutes, but finally the phone sex gods delivered us a woman who could do Italian fuck talk. I'm not sure if she was talking about fucking her neighbor or reading the phone book, but it sounded hot. We put her on speaker phone and sprawled out in our suite, her voice our soundtrack as we drank orange-tasting liqueur until we nearly passed out.

Dee, however, wasn't satisfied. At some ridiculous hour, he perked up, his drink clenched in his fist.

"Oy, are we rock stars or are we wankers?" he says.

I lift my glass and slur, "Dude, we're fucking rock stars."

So we trashed the place. We broke some glasses, pissed on the floor, just juvenile shit. I passed out on a ripped mattress. I remember this point clearly because I had mattress stuffing in my nose when a man in a little red hotel vest woke me. He looked grave.

"Your guests are here, sir."

Antonio was in the lobby. My Italian phone sex lover had fled and the phone was thrumming out its pleading signal to hang it up, sending echoes of her panting breath in my head, pounding like a dirge. I sincerely wished I had not drunk so much. But too bad—it was game time.

We threw cold water on our faces and tried hand smoothing out the wrinkles in our slept-in suits. We needed a shave. We needed lots of things. No time.

"Let's get this over with," I said.

The elevator operator, greeting us with a wide toothy grin, opened the door for us. He looked like an organ grinder monkey. I was about to tell him this when the elevator opened to the lobby.

Buon giorno, heroes. It's Antonio time.

He didn't look like the guy in his mother's tratorria or an opera enthusiast. The silk scarf and linen slacks were long gone, replaced by a dark suit, his eyes shaded by dark glasses. Flanking him were two guys, beefy men straight out of a Hollywood gangster movie. Each was handcuffed to a suitcase. Their tan leather gun holders peeked out from unbuttoned sports jackets.

The lark was over. I was scared to fucking death.

Antonio gave me a hard look. "Why are you both down here? We must be to your room."

We all crammed into a little European elevator and rode up in silence. Back in our room, the two big guys scanned the broken glass and mattress stuffing and briefly caught each other's eye. As if they hadn't already sized us up, it was now confirmed: we were amateurs. One of the men calmly walked through each room in the suite and turned on every TV. He picked CNN and cranked the volume up loud. Real loud. The other methodically shut all the curtains. The room was now dark except for the flickering lights of the televisions. All of this happened slowly.

Antonio breaks the silence and says, in Italian, what I assume to be "Put the money on the bed."

We walk to the master bedroom, and both men open their suitcases and slowly stack the money on the bed, which takes forever. Antonio waits. I wanted to break the tension with an opera joke or something but just kept my mouth shut.

When his men were done, Antonio says, "Count it."

Trying my damnedest to sound conciliatory, I say, "It's cool, man. I trust you. Let's get out of here, you know?"

"Count it."

So Dee and I stand next to the bed and count the money. CNN is blaring. My mouth was dry, and I could see Dee's hands trembling.

Dee says, "It's all here."

Antonio and I begin stuffing the money into our backpack. We had brought along dirty laundry to pile on top of the cash, but the hard angles of the stacks were bulging against the sides of the bag, making it ridiculously square and bulky. Put the money in a fucking backpack: Whose idea was that? Oh . . . right.

But hey, we had the money.

Antonio was curt, all business. His orders were as follows: we were to drive directly to the Austrian border. His men would follow. We must not stop. At the border, we'd be on our own.

We took the elevator back to the lobby. At the hotel's double-doored exit, I held one door for Antonio's men while, at the same time, they held the other door for me. Confused, we all tried to go out at the same time and bumped our way to the sidewalk. It was kind of funny, except for the guns. Dee and I took to the street at a brisk but controlled gait, got into our Skoda, and drove directly to the border, checking our rearview mirrors obsessively to make sure our guides were a) still there and b) not going to ambush us on some empty country road. The drive, thankfully, was uneventful. At the border, the guards just waved us through. Goodbye, henchmen; hello (almost), Heroville. We were still stressed, but at least we weren't dead.

We pulled off the road at a little Austrian diner and got some sausages, juice, and coffee. With the toughest part of our journey behind us, my sphincter unclenched a bit. After a few nerve-calming cigarettes, we got back on the road. All was well until we crested a hill in the Austrian Alps and Dee starts stomping on the clutch, muttering "fucking hell." There's a grinding sound, soon joined by a metallic smell. It was a Sunday, mid-morning, in the dead of winter, and suddenly two hungover and scared young men with $250,000 in cash in a backpack found themselves stranded in a dead Skoda.

Leaving the car on the side of the road, we stuck our thumbs out and hitched a ride to the nearest village in the back of a Euro-van delivery truck, the heavy backpack slung tightly over Dee's shoulders. We found a mechanic who informed us, in broken English, that the only man with the parts and know-how to repair our vehicle was out of town until tomorrow morning. We'd have to stay the night. There were no hotels, but that was okay: the repairman knew the woman who ran the local equestrian stables. "Those horses, they sleeps better than us do," he says.

He took us to the stables and explained our predicament to the woman, who agreed to let us stay the night.

Inside the horse stables, I found a seat in some hay with a view of the nearby mountains. The caper was losing its luster. Catching my breath, I remembered a conversation I'd had with Erika just a few days earlier. We had taken a hard look at the lifestyle we had created for ourselves. It wasn't just the drugs, though at some point we knew we couldn't keep up this pace without some serious negative repercussions. We were engaged. This was a real relationship. I was about to turn thirty. And like a lot of folks at the end of their carefree first decade of adulthood, I was starting to wonder where all this was heading.

A career. It took me a long time to figure it out, but that's what I wanted. And Erika, she wanted the same thing—to work hard at something, for a long time. But what? And how? It certainly wasn't going to be at the Terminal Bar, not anymore. This money we were smuggling, I just wanted to drop it off, save Katka's life, and move on. That dream that had sustained me was just that: a dream. I just wanted this shit to be done.

All those times I'd moved as a kid, followed by college, moving abroad, squatting and grifting . . . it had left me tired. I wanted a home, a place to settle in. And deep down, I knew Prague was not home, not really. It was just another cool place.

My adrenaline was wearing off and my nerves were shot. Dee, seeing this, tried to lighten the mood.

"I've got a solution to this shit," he says.

He pulls out a camera, unzips the backpack and turns it over, sending the stacks of money thumping on the barn floor. With only time on our hands, we start taking photos of us and the money. We stack it next to the horses and on hay bales. We undress and roll naked in it. We walk to a local restaurant for dinner where we go into the bathroom and pile the money atop a urinal. We get a great shot in front of a *wiener haus* sign.

After dinner we buy a bottle of Jägermeister from the restaurant bar and hang out at the stables, telling stories and smoking cigarettes. In many ways the situation we were in was still dangerous and not that much fun anymore. But under our horse blankets, snuggling $250,000, listening to Dee tell me some bawdy story, I never felt better in my life.

The next day, our fix-it man arrived. Bad news: it was the transmission. Repairing it could take days, and time was running out: the Skoda was toast. Taking pity on us, the repairman said his nephew could give us a lift to the train station. "And hurry. The only daily train leaves in thirty minutes."

The nephew pulls up in a hot rod, blasting the German metal band Rammstein. Delighted, we jump in and he peels out of the parking lot. But again, our luck runs out. Around a corner a flock of sheep blocks the road. We miss the train. At the station we say goodbye to the nephew and find seats in a sterile coffee shop. What now? Planes and trains were out of the question. We'd have to rent a car. But first—with several borders still to cross—it was time to get cleaned up.

We went to a department store and purchased new, normal suits and a toiletry kit. In a mall bathroom, we shaved our faces clean. We popped out Dee's infected eyebrow piercing and covered it with a band-aid. We separated the money and put it in two smaller, more reasonable-looking sports duffel bags. We found a rental car outlet and—why not?—upgraded to a BMW with the Italians' cash.

With our fancy car and hurried makeovers, we actually looked pretty sharp. But the romp was getting old. And we both knew that the Czech border lay hours ahead. Honestly, before all this other bullshit happened, it was the hurdle I'd worried most about anyway.

As we neared the Czech border, I remember popping in a Ministry cassette tape. I thought the dark and heavy music would fit the scene perfectly. I was also very nervous and more than a little manic and couldn't seem to stop talking.

But Dee was stressed.

"Shut. The fuck. Up!"

I didn't blame him. I must have been driving him crazy.

"Turn off that fucking music and don't say another word."

"Ok, man, cool."

"And give me that soda."

A can of Coke was rolling around on the car floor. I hand it to him, he opens it. It explodes in his face, of course, and all over the driver's side window.

The line moves forward and here comes an armed Czech border guard, his Russian-made machine gun slung lazily over his hip like he couldn't care less either way.

"Papers."

—*mm*—

There's this Czech surrealist filmmaker named Jan Svankmajer. His films are partly animated, partly dark, and 100 percent bizarre. From the moment the Czech guard asked Dee and me for our papers I felt I'd entered one of his films. I can see it now, the camera zooming in for a tight shot of soda dripping from Dee's band-aid on his eyebrow. Reflected in the drip is the border guard sporting an out-of-date USSR uniform, the hammer and sickle covered with black tape. The word "papers" is an echoing, physical menace, peering down on us like a bored vulture, waiting for an answer.

But then the air changes. Sounds suddenly erupt from the guard booths. Yelling turns to chaos that turns to chanting that will soon turn to fireworks. We catch a few words: *Ledni. Czech. Hokej. Gol.* The Czech Republic had just won the World Championship in hockey. The guard's attention shifts to the celebration and quietly, with our balls resuming their pre-terrorized shape in our scrotums, we calmly drive away.

We passed through the East European side of the border, which, as always, was a mad place, a schemers' paradise. Bored truck drivers waiting days for some unknown stamp. Hitchhikers. Prostitutes in leg warmers and aerobic wear. Gypsy peddlers. On my other trips through these in-between places, I found the macabre circus-like scenes romantic as a fairy tale. But on this day, these were the people with whom I felt a kinship, and it made me sad. And so very tired. I saw a man selling garden gnomes with a transistor radio to his ear. He smiled at me as we weaved out of the chaos.

Two more hours in our Beemer and we were finally, blessedly, in Prague, which by then was in full impromptu celebration mode. We dropped off the car, gripped our bags tightly, and walked through throngs of drunken revelers shooting bottle rockets, celebrating their hockey team. Gunpowder filled the air, and tracers of light tattooed my retinas. Two men hugging fell laughing in the street in front of us.

As we neared Mark's flat on Old Town Square, some unnamed chip I'd been carrying on my shoulder for days, if not years, fell away, and the magic around me turned to something else—litanies:

The blood of Jesus and northeast Ohio steel mills. Whores and lithium. Wrestling with angels.

Veganism and LSD. Hitchhiking and saving the trees. My fist in the air.

Meth nosebleeds and voices in my head. Tattoos and bed spins. Being hung over.

I was done with this shit. All of it.

As Dee rang the bell to Mark's flat, I knew the truth. I would not see the Terminal Bar open. In only a few months I would take my only treasure, Erika, and make a new life in America.

I felt changed. Like my wanderings were over.

As Mark opened his door, I shut my eyes, leaned my head back, and felt the snow flakes melt on my face. I took one last deep breath of Prague magic. When I opened my eyes again, I was gone.

Afterword

*   *   *   *   *
   *   *   *   *   *
*   *   *   *   *

Chuck?

I left Prague only a few months after smuggling the money. Mark started drinking again and essentially tucked his tail between his legs and scurried away, but Dee, to his credit, took over where I'd left off. The money worked: Katka lived, and within months, Dee opened the Terminal Bar and ran it swimmingly. It became a successful business that also ran the largest private internet service provider in the country.

Not long after I was fired from EYFA, the record label I started went on to produce numerous and award-winning world music albums. The Peace Circus, bereft of its leader, became an employee collective and toured Europe for almost a decade, with Litti as its manager.

Less than a year after we left Europe for America, Erika and I were married in a greenhouse in St. Louis. I stopped doing hard drugs. I found a couple of jobs in Chicago, one as a boy Friday for a jingle-writing company and another leading tours about the city's history and architecture on a double-decker bus. Pretty quickly, I created a career in public broadcasting. I hosted a TV show for Wisconsin Public Television for five years and landed a producer gig for one of the national shows on public radio, *To the Best of Our Knowledge*, where I eventually became an on-air talent on the show and even nabbed a Peabody Award. I still do this job today.

For more than a decade I have been in Madison, Wisconsin. Small-town living and career stability turned into gym memberships and a beautiful little house with a view of a lake and two wonderful young children—Odin and Vivian. Every Thursday I throw back a few at my local tavern with a group of fellow dads, maybe spark up a joint in the parking lot. This is my life now, and it is good. It is all something I didn't even know I could have, or should have, dreamed of.

The others are doing well, too. Dee got married and has a child. Antony and Marketa are still married and are raising a child as well. Paxus is living in a commune in Virginia, still fighting the good fight. Litti and Ingrid and Stephanie and Erma—I'm Facebook friends with all of them, and they are all doing amazing and interesting things. Any bridges I thought I burned are apparently mended.

Mark passed away while I was working on this book. RIP.

—ᵐᵐ—

So why did I write this book?

Several years ago, after roughly fifteen years free from any psychiatric medication, I awoke one night with a start. This was not that unusual: Erika and I had young children, after all, who would regularly roust us from sleep after a nightmare or because they needed a drink or a hug. But this time, the house was quiet. And then they came. It was the voices, speaking to me in their familiar gibberish. Just like when I was a child, I found myself traveling, skimming the water, headed to "the Island." I have heard voices my whole life, but the familiarity of these had me in a cold sweat—they seemed more intimate. I went to the dining room table to have a drink of water, to sit, and to think. The intensity and volume of the voices in my head had me dizzy. Then it happened. Silence. Its suddenness was even more fearful than the cacophony that preceded it. But it wasn't long until "the Source" spoke. Not the faint, repeated "Chuck?" I had learned to ignore years ago. This was different. This was loud and clear. A terrifying evolution that sent me to the corner of the room, crouching and in tears.

"Jump! Jump, Chuck."

"Jump! Jump, Chuck!"

It didn't stop. And I realized it wasn't going to.

Erika came down, and crouching beside me, held me. It was clear I needed help.

But, once again, I tried my best to ignore it. I took some time off from work. I smoked a lot of pot. I began working out more rigorously at one of those gyms where you jump on boxes and crawl on all fours and do pull-ups until your arms hang limp. At night I started going the megadose-of-oxycodone route and had fitful nights of unspeakable nightmares. I'd awake in a manic state, unable to control my emotions. The commands continued like Dick and Jane on acid:

"Jump! Jump, Chuck!"

"Hide! Hide, Chuck!"

"Run! Run, Chuck!"

This, as you can imagine, left me a wreck. And that's when "the conversation" happened. I call it that because it is forever burned into my heart. Erika sat me down and told me she no longer felt comfortable leaving me alone with the children. I was too erratic. Too goddamn angry. The rubber had truly met the road.

We considered having me committed. We called the hotline. But it was the expected bullshit. "Are you a danger to yourself or others?" Who fucking asks a question like that and expects an honest answer?

"Jump! Jump, Chuck!"

"Run! Run, Chuck!"

This is the moment when Chuck could become Bob. I have always harbored a great fear of that man. What did he used to do for a living? Was his wife hot? Did he help his kids with their homework? When did he become unsafe to be around? How did it all fall apart?

I immediately entered intensive therapy and sat down with my nemesis: a psychiatrist.

After a few sessions my doctor laid it out. First, I didn't have schizophrenia. That diagnosis was thrown around a lot back then, he said, as were the meds to treat it. The doses were too big and too strong. He formally diagnosed me with bipolar 1 disorder. My voices do come from psychosis, from extremes of mania, he explained. They are hallucinations. But with a schizophrenic those hallucinations are indiscernible from reality. I was never delusional. I always knew that the voices in my head were just that, in my head. But still, there they were.

So, after trying out a host of medications and doses, we landed on aripiprazole and, yes, lithium. My daily doses were back, and with them returned all the old doubts.

My positive energy, my outgoing personality, my desire to talk, my extroverted need of others . . . these were all things that made me, well, me. Was all of that just a manifestation of my mania, a mania now medicated away? And if so, was I gone now too?

And what about all those years of Christianity and my extreme drug use? Were those just the misunderstandings of a mentally ill person trying to make sense of his own brain? And now that I understand the brain as electricity and chemicals (mine being a tad off), does that mean that those transcendent experiences and memories and life lessons were meaningless?

I felt a sadness, a mourning, for this horrible cancer that I finally decided to have removed, as if it were something to miss. As if IT was me. "Chuck?" was now a question I was asking myself.

But there was one question I wasn't asking: Should I stop taking these meds? I am committed to staying on them this time, and not just for my family but for myself.

Every morning, I pop two 300mg lithium pills into my palm, toss them in my mouth, and chase them with water from the sink. Every night I take two more, along with one 20mg aripiprazole pill. They're in the medicine cabinet, up where my kids can't reach them. Mostly, I don't even think about it. I just take them. But occasionally you can't avoid it: you see yourself in the bathroom mirror. And I'll be honest, at times it still bothers me. But at this point, I'm a lot more thankful and a lot less angry.

When I first started taking my meds again, I'd meet with a therapist and talk a mile a minute, trying to get to the bottom of all of this. She laughed and told me to slow down. But I couldn't. So she recommended I write it, my mental illness story. Just write it all down.

So I did. I wrote it all down.

This is my book, filled with flawed, exaggerated, scary, romantic, asinine, beautiful, and at times magnificent stories.

So, why did I write this book? Simply put, because "Chuck?" doesn't scare me anymore.

Epilogue

*   *   *   *   *
  *   *   *   *
*   *   *   *   *

A Bunny Floating by
on a Balloon Eating
a Magic Hot Dog

Once upon a time there was a little boy named Odin and a little girl named Vivian. Together they had many great adventures. This is just one of them.

Odin and Vivian were at a baseball game with their daddy. It was a beautiful sunny day, and there was a gentle breeze carrying the smell of mowed grass and popcorn to their outfield seats. In the third inning, a batter struck a home-run ball. It headed right for them. Odin and Vivian stretched out their arms to catch the ball and, as luck would have it, they caught it at the same time. Nearby fans gave them high-fives. Their daddy took their picture and gave them kisses. But then something changed, something in the sky. All the grown-ups went back to watching the game and didn't notice. But Odin and Vivian did.

Far off in the distance, a dark shape was floating over the stadium. At first they thought it was a faraway plane or maybe an eagle, but as it got closer Odin and Vivian saw what it was. It was a Bunny Floating by on a Balloon Eating a Magic Hot Dog. And it was headed right for them.

Then Daddy noticed the Bunny Floating by on a Balloon Eating a Magic Hot Dog, too.

"Your catch must have conjured up some magic," he told Odin and Vivian. "You can say hi to the bunny, *but do not eat the hot dog*. It is magic. And everyone knows that magic hot dogs, especially when being eaten by bunnies floating on balloons, are

183

bad news." A number of grown-ups seated nearby nodded in agreement.

But did Odin and Vivian listen? No. No they did not.

As soon as the Bunny Floating by on a Balloon Eating a Magic Hot Dog got near enough, Odin grabbed the hot dog. He ate the bun. Vivian ate the meat. And the Bunny Floating by on a Balloon Eating a Magic Hot Dog, along with Daddy and everyone else in the baseball stadium, stopped and stared at them.

And then it happened.

Vivian said it first. "I'm hungry."

"Me too," said Odin.

So they started to eat. And eat and eat and eat and eat. They ate their seats. They ate more seats. In a frenzy, they ate a soda vendor. They paused to burp, then turned to look at their daddy, and they ate him, too. They ate everyone. They ate the baseball stadium. They ate the parking lot, the trees, the signs, the roads. They ate the town. They drank a lake. They burped some more, and then they ate some more—animals, volcanoes, the oceans. They turned the North and South poles into slushies. Soon they were floating in outer space. They had eaten the entire world.

"I wonder if the moon is really made out of cheese?" Odin asked Vivian.

"I'm hungry," said Vivian.

Within minutes, the moon was gone. (It was *not* made out of cheese, by the way.)

Next the stars. The planets. Odin drank the Milky Way while Vivian, who likes spicy food, devoured the sun.

Soon, there was nothing left. Just two very fat and hungry children floating in nothingness. And they started to look at each other.

Soon, far off in the distance, something appeared in the nothingness. At first it looked like a faraway plane or maybe an eagle. But that couldn't be right; Odin and Vivian had already eaten all of those. But as it got closer Odin and Vivian saw what it was. It was a Bunny Floating by on a Balloon Eating a Magic Hot Dog. And the Bunny Floating by on a Balloon Eating a Magic Hot Dog was headed straight for them.

The Bunny Floating by on a Balloon Eating a Magic Hot Dog stopped in front of Odin and Vivian. They both started to cry. "We're sorry," they said. The Bunny Floating by on a Balloon Eating a Magic Hot Dog was very angry. But the Bunny Floating by on a Balloon Eating a Magic Hot Dog knew Odin and Vivian were sorry. And they certainly looked silly—all fat and spinning in nothingness. The Bunny Floating by on a Balloon Eating a Magic Hot Dog asked them if there was anything left. Was there anything left that they had not eaten?

"We ate everything," Vivian said sadly.

Suddenly Odin remembered that the ball he and Vivian had caught was still in his pocket. He showed it to the Bunny Floating by on a Balloon Eating a Magic Hot Dog.

"Perfect," said the Bunny Floating by on a Balloon Eating a Magic Hot Dog. And the Bunny Floating by on a Balloon Eating a Magic Hot Dog threw it as hard as the Bunny Floating by on a Balloon Eating a Magic Hot Dog could. Jupiter reappeared. The ball came back, and the Bunny Floating by on a Balloon Eating a Magic Hot Dog threw it again—Mars. Again, the moon. Again and again and again and again until the every last tree and chipmunk were back.

Well, almost everything was back.

The Bunny Floating by on a Balloon Eating a Magic Hot Dog handed Odin and Vivian the baseball. The Bunny Floating by on a Balloon Eating a Magic Hot Dog told them to close their eyes and count to three. And the Bunny Floating by on a Balloon Eating a Magic Hot Dog told them to grab the ball together and throw it as far as the east is to the west.

"One! Two! Three!" Odin and Vivian yelled. And together they threw the ball.

When Odin and Vivian woke the next morning, they both had a strange taste in their mouths. Neither one touched their breakfast. When Daddy asked what was wrong, Odin and Vivian looked at each other and shrugged.

"I'm just not hungry, I guess," Odin said.

"Me, neither," Vivian added.

And they went out to play.